P9-BIM-397

Entertaining the world
P. T. BARNUM

Britannica Bookshelf—Great Lives for Young Americans

Entertaining the world

P. T. BARNUM

By Fred J. Cook

Illustrated by Dan Siculan

Published by

ENCYCLOPAEDIA BRITANNICA PRESS, *Chicago*

COPYRIGHT © 1962 BY ENCYCLOPAEDIA BRITANNICA
LIBRARY OF CONGRESS CATALOG NUMBER 62-10425
PRINTED IN THE UNITED STATES OF AMERICA

Copyright under International Copyright Union
All Rights Reserved under Pan American and Universal Copyright Conventions

TABLE OF CONTENTS

Entertaining the world
P. T. BARNUM

Chapter 1

The Great Show Begins

His name was Phineas Taylor Barnum. He was born in the little country town of Bethel, Connecticut, just too late to witness his first great show on earth—the fireworks of the Fourth of July, 1810. It was virtually the last great show that Barnum ever missed. For he was to become "the prince of showmen"; the entertainer of kings and queens; the magical master of the Barnum and Bailey Circus, "The Greatest Show on Earth."

A boy born to farm chores, Barnum bounded out of the lonely Connecticut hills to dazzle the world's millions and make his name a household word on two continents. BARNUM. More than a century and a half after he was born, the very name still has magic and mystery in it. To generations who have been thrilled by the circus, the name Barnum has stood like a signpost at the gateway to the world of the marvelous.

How did it ever happen? How could this obscure Yankee, born in the remoteness of rural Connecticut, seize the world's stage for himself and make himself at home on it?

Barnum was born into an age of fakery and a family of fakers. His life began with a practical jest designed to teach him that things are not what they seem. It was a lesson that Barnum never forgot; indeed, he turned it into a formula for fortune.

The boy was named after his grandfather on his mother's side, Phineas Taylor, and old Phineas, as Barnum later wrote, "would go farther, wait longer, work harder, and contrive deeper, to carry out a practical joke, than for anything else under heaven." The day that Barnum was christened, his grandfather began to contrive. Gravely, he presented his little namesake with a "gift-deed" conveying to him five acres of land lying east of the village and known as "Ivy Island." Almost the first thing that Barnum realized when he became old enough to understand was that he, tiny as he was, was a landowner. Since wealth in those days was measured largely by the amount of land a man owned, young Barnum was led to believe that he had received an exceptionally fine start in life as the result of his grandfather's generosity.

There was much joshing among the family and neighbors about Barnum's five-acre "estate"; and the boy himself, taking it all seriously, was puffed up at times with pardonable pride at his own good fortune. It was not, however, until he was ten years old that he actually first saw "the broad acres" his grandfather had deeded him. Then he discovered that "Ivy Island" was a worthless swamp, the home of snakes and poison ivy vines—and that all the talk about it over the years had been a cruel jest at his expense.

Disappointment and the discovery that he had been the butt of a long-standing neighborhood joke might have shamed another boy and left a life long scar. But it was not so with Barnum. Young as he was, he too was a practical joker; he understood the rough country humor of his times. And so he chalked his "Ivy Island" lesson up to experience; and when he became a man, he was to pretend, just as his grandfather had pretended, that "Ivy Island" represented landed estate. Finding a businessman who knew no better, just as he had known no better, he was to use the "estate" to lay the groundwork for his fortune.

Fortune certainly did not run in his family. His father, Philo F. Barnum, had spent a lifetime trying a variety of occupations and had found none particularly rewarding. He had been a tailor, farmer, tavern-keeper, livery-stable proprietor, country storekeeper, and operator of a small express company. When young Phineas, as he later wrote, made his "debut" on the morning of July 5, 1810, his father was farming, and his small income had to be stretched to meet the needs of a large household. By his first wife, who had died, Philo Barnum had had five children, and Phineas was the first of five to be born to his second wife. Ten children underfoot made a crowded, but a decidedly merry home.

Barnum's father had "a lively turn of mind and relished a joke better than the average of mankind"; but it was his mother's father, the canny and practical-joking Phineas Taylor, who exerted the greatest influence on the boy. His grandfather on his father's side, Ephraim Barnum, had been a captain in the militia during the Revolution, but he appeared in Barnum's later recollections as a pale shadow beside the fond memories of Phineas Taylor.

Barnum was not only the namesake, but the much-favored grandson of Phineas Taylor. Phineas' face was the first that Barnum remembered recognizing; and during the boy's first six years of his life, his grandfather carried him everywhere and treated him to lump sugar he always kept handy in his pockets. Phineas Taylor eagerly began to teach his favorite grandson the value of money, and Barnum's strongly developed instinct for acquiring satisfying amounts of this valuable commodity seems to have stemmed, in large part at least, from his grandfather's tutoring.

The grandfather was constantly donating pennies to the boy to buy raisins and candies; and, as soon as Barnum was old enough to understand, Phineas Taylor used the pennies as a device to bring him up properly in the hard, shrewd school of Yankee bargaining. Always haggle with the storekeeper, he instructed the boy; always make sure you get "the lowest cash price."

By such tightfisted methods, Barnum was encouraged not just to spend but to save. By the time he was six years old, he had stored up enough pennies to make a whole dollar. He did not quite understand what this meant; but his grandfather told him that, if he would put all his coins together and go with him, he would show little Barnum "something worth having." Curious to see what this might be, Barnum wrapped his hoarded wealth into a handkerchief and accompanied his grandfather to the village tavern, whose proprietor was Stiles Wakelee.

"Here, Mr. Wakelee, is the richest boy in this part of

the country," Phineas Taylor told the tavern keeper. "He has a dollar in cash. I wish you to take his change and give him a silver dollar for it."

The tavern-keeper completed the transaction, and Barnum never got over it. He never forgot the feel of that first "monstrous big silver dollar." "Talk of 'cart-wheels,'" Barnum later wrote, "there never was one half so huge as that dollar looked to me. I believed, without the slightest reservation, that this entire earth and all its contents could be purchased by that wonderful piece of bullion, and that it would be a bad bargain at that."

Not unnaturally, the boy developed a desire to experience this wonderful thrill again and again. His mother, who was "close" as the country expression goes, encouraged him to keep saving pennies. Soon Barnum began to dream up schemes of his own to increase his hoard. At an astonishingly early age, he sensed the opportunity that an enterprising individual might find in large crowds. An event that remained long in his memory occurred in the fall of 1817, when he was only a little more than seven. There was to be a hanging in nearby Danbury; and country folk from miles around flocked to see it. Barnum climbed a tree and watched it all; what seemed to impress him most was not the death of the murderer who was hanged, but the size of the throng. People obviously would gather in great numbers if the attraction that drew them was unusual enough; and where people assembled in great numbers, there was money—and the chance to transfer some of it to one's own pockets.

Barnum thought about this, and he soon hit upon a plan to test his theory. In those days the local militia were the backbone of national defense, and the militiamen gathered for drill on regular "training days." Barnum decided there must be some way to lure some of the plentiful pennies out of the pockets of the amateur soldiers. Obtaining a gallon of molasses, he boiled it down and worked it into molasses candy. Then, on training day, he peddled his candy among the militiamen and came away a dollar richer. He used this newfound capital to broaden his stock and get more things to sell. Soon, in addition to the molasses candy, he was peddling gingerbread, cookies, sugar candies, and best of all, cherry rum—a concoction consisting of a demijohn of New England rum, a quantity of wild cherries, and some sugar.

"I soon learned that the soldiers were good cherry-rum customers," Barnum later wrote, "and no sooner did I learn the words 'Halt. Ground arms,' than I approached the 'trainers' with my decanter and wine-glass."

Barnum made so much money on training days that, by the time he was ten, he seemed almost on the road to wealth. But then, as he wrote, his father "considerately allowed me to purchase my own clothing," and this "kept my pile reduced to moderate size." Nevertheless, young Barnum kept a sharp eye out "for the main chance"; and by the time he was twelve, he had acquired a sheep of his own and a calf and some other property. He was, he felt, "quite a man of substance."

This substance had all been acquired by mental agility rather than by hard labor. Barnum heartily disliked the farm and its never ending chores. "My father insisted that I could hoe and plough and dig in the garden as well as anybody else," he wrote, "but I generally contrived to shirk the work altogether." In the little town of Bethel, this distaste for the gritty and backbreaking toil on the land soon gave young Phineas Barnum the reputation of being the laziest boy in town. Yet he wasn't actually lazy, except when it came to doing things he disliked.

He was a bright student. He began to go to school when he was six. In those days, school was a terrifying experience. Teachers were tyrants who used ferules, birch rods, and rattan canes to whip their pupils into proper obedience. Each school had a dark hole of a closet in which the worst offenders were made to stand as punishment for their misdeeds. Barnum suffered the usual penalties meted out to all schoolboys in that day. On one occasion a teacher picked up a ruler and threw it at his head. Barnum ducked and the ruler cracked across the face of the girl sitting behind him. Gravely, the teacher told her that he would give her credit for this undeserved blow and would skip the next punishment she was certain soon to deserve.

In his studies, Barnum was especially strong in one subject. It was, as might be expected, arithmetic. He could outfigure any other boy in Bethel, and his teacher became so confident of his ability that, on one occasion, a bet was made. The teacher wagered with a neighbor that young Phineas Barnum, then only 12 years old, could figure the correct number of feet in a load of wood in five minutes.

It was late at night when the bet was made, and Barnum was in bed. This made no difference. The matter had to be settled on the spot; and so the teacher and the neighbor went to Barnum's home, routed him out of bed, and explained the problem. Barnum marked down the dimensions of the wagon with a piece of chalk on the stovepipe in his father's kitchen, did some rapid calculations, and in just two minutes came up with the right answer. Never did a student find a better way to get into the good graces of his teacher. Barnum's instructor pocketed his winnings and went away beaming. The neighbor who had lost was left poorer and completely astonished, a condition that was to become quite common to those who crossed the path of Phineas Barnum in later years.

Smart as Barnum was, however, he was only twelve years old. There were others in the world shrewder and wilier than he—a truth he was now to learn the hard way when he made his first excursion into the great world outside Bethel. Late one afternoon in January, 1822, Daniel Brown, of Southbury, Connecticut, arrived at the village tavern, then being run by Philo Barnum. Brown had a drove of fat cattle that he was taking to New York. After his stock had been put in the barnyard, and while he warmed himself before the tavern fire, he remarked that he intended to pick up some more cattle en route. He could use a smart boy to help him keep them from straying. The smart boy, who was then present, pricked up his ears at this remark and hurried to get his father to recommend him.

So it was that when Daniel Brown started off at daybreak in the midst of a driving snowstorm, Phineas Barnum went with him. A short distance from Bethel, Barnum's horse slipped and fell, and Barnum sprained his ankle. Despite the pain, Barnum kept quiet about his injury for fear that he might be sent home at once and so miss his chance to "go to York," an adventure in those days of limited travel that seemed as romantic to a boy from Bethel as a trip to the South Seas might seem today. Limping when he had to walk, the boy gritted his teeth and kept going with the herd. It took four days to complete the drive over snowy roads, but finally Brown and his young helper reached the city and put up at the Bull's Head Tavern.

It would take about a week to sell all the cattle. While Brown was busy with this task, Phineas Barnum was free to explore the wonders of New York. Before he left home, his mother had provided him with a dollar in spending money. This, to the boy, represented a fortune with which, it seemed, virtually any treasure in the world might be bought. Rich, then, in his own estimation at least, he set out to see what New York might have to offer. Not far from the Bull's Head Tavern, he discovered a most wonderful shop. It had a wide variety of things to sell, but what promptly caught the ravenous eye of young Barnum was a display of oranges. Fresh oranges were a rarity in Bethel; Barnum had never been able to get his fill of them. Now was his chance. He entered the shop and asked the saleslady how much the oranges cost.

"Four pence apiece," she replied.

In Connecticut four pence meant six cents. Taking it for granted that the meaning was the same in New York and practicing the technique his grandfather had taught him of always bargaining for the best cash price, Barnum promptly protested.

"That seems like too high a price to me," he said. "I'll give you ten cents for two." Since in New York four pence

[*17*]

meant four pennies, and not six, Barnum was really offering
the woman two cents more than she had asked. Naturally
she let him argue her into accepting his terms. The first
two oranges were so good that Barnum promptly purchased

Young Barnum found a world of wonders in a New York shop.

two more. When these had been consumed, he decided that
he had had enough oranges for the moment; and he began
to examine the other wares in the shop. He discovered all
kinds of marvels. There was a little gun that would shoot a
stick across a room, something that no boy in Bethel had

ever seen; there were torpedoes that would go off with a loud bang if you hurled them against the wall or floor; there was a watch, a breastpin, a top. One by one, Barnum bought them all. When he had finished, he still had 11 cents left, a sum great enough, he thought, for all his other wants.

Soon the wonderful gadgets that he had purchased began to get him into trouble. He discharged his gun in the crowded barroom of the tavern; its stick grazed a customer's nose and smacked the bartender above the eye. The bartender let out an angry roar, grabbed young Barnum, shook him till his teeth rattled, then boxed his ears. The boy was still smarting from this experience when curiosity about the way his torpedoes worked became too much for him. He hurled a couple against the wall just as the tavern's guests were going in to dinner, and the landlord, even more indignant than the bartender had been, came rushing out and knocked him over backwards with one swipe of his hand. Picking himself up, Barnum retired to his room to sulk and nurse his injured feelings. The dawn of a new day found him revived and right back in the toy shop again.

This time he spotted the most wonderful gadget of all, one that he simply had to have—a knife with two blades, a gimlet, and a corkscrew. But it cost 31 cents, and he had only 11 cents left. There was only one way to get the knife. He would have to trade some of his recent purchases back to the saleslady who had been so willing to take ten cents instead of eight for two oranges. She was eager to oblige him; but she pointed out that he was now dealing in secondhand goods and that she could take them back only at a discount. Barnum agreed, and so he acquired the knife.

[*19*]

Hardly had he obtained possession of it, however, before he made another discovery. The shop had molasses candy for sale. Barnum was an expert on molasses candy, but this was nothing like the product that he had peddled to the training militia on Bethel muster days. This was whiter, smoother, much more delicious. It was so good that once he started to eat it, he couldn't stop. One by one he traded back all his possessions for the molasses candy, even the wonderful new knife. Still Barnum, who was broke by now, yearned for more. His mother, when he left home, had provided him with a couple of handkerchiefs and an extra pair of socks. Barnum was sure he would never have any use for these articles. So he traded them in for more molasses candy. Only when he had finally eaten his way through this last purchase did he stop—and then only because he had nothing left to trade.

In this impoverished state, he returned home to Bethel. His brothers and sisters were heartbroken because he had brought no presents for them from the wonderful city of York. His mother, examining his depleted wardrobe, was outraged. The missing handkerchiefs and socks, the final sacrifices to his gluttony, stirred her to fury. She promptly whipped him and put him to bed. Thus, in deep disgrace, ended Barnum's first great adventure in the outside world. He had fallen a victim to his own piggish appetite. He had been "taken." But he had "been to York," something that no other boy in Bethel could boast; and the wonder of it lived on in his mind. Some day he would go back.

Chapter **2**

Rising Young Merchant

About a year after Barnum's disastrous sampling of the wares of the New York toy shop, his father decided to put him on the other side of the counter in a country store in Bethel. All other efforts to find work to which young Phineas would take kindly had failed. He invented more ways to get out of doing farm chores than it seemed possible for one boy to dream up. Philo Barnum, in final desperation, erected a small building in Bethel; took Hiram Weed for his partner; and laid in a stock of dry goods, groceries, and hardware, the typically varied commodities of a general store. When the store opened, thirteen-year-old Phineas Barnum was installed as its clerk.

From the first, Barnum felt proud of his new position. Of course he had to take down and put up shutters, sweep out the store, and build and tend the fire. These were dreary chores of the type he detested, but there were compensations in the store as there were not on the farm. Barnum liked to strut behind the counter, a pen stuck behind his ear. He liked to make entries in the important-looking ledger. He relished waiting on the women of the town and engaging in the sharp battle of wits that accompanied the trade of produce—butter, eggs, beeswax, feathers—for some of the store's commodities. Soon, in addition to all this, he developed another and more personal interest. His father and Weed agreed to let him put in his own stock of candies to sell to the youngsters of the town. Soon Barnum, ever with that eye "for the main chance," was spending almost as much time at his own private candy counter as he was waiting on customers who wanted to buy more important and more costly items.

Tending a country store in those days provided a liberal education in the motives of people and the general contrariness of mankind. The storekeeper and his customers engaged in a constant battle of wits to see who could get the best of the other. It was a contest in which each side, by a kind of mutual understanding, was on guard every step of the way; and so no trick was considered too low, no stratagem really dishonest. It was simply up to one person to see that the other didn't get away with whatever it was he was trying to pull off. If one person was asleep and didn't protect his own interests, that was his fault. Since cash was extremely scarce in those days and credit exceptionally risky, most of the trade of the store was carried on by barter. And in bartering the storekeeper had to watch out.

Country women brought in bundles of rags to exchange for goods. They swore that the bundles contained nothing but linen and cotton goods; but when Barnum opened the bundles, he often found the centers packed with stones, gravel, or ashes. A farmer came in with a load of oats, corn, or rye. There would be 60 bushels there, he would say; but when Barnum counted, he might find only 55. When such discrepancies were called to the customers' attention, the women with the stone-stuffed bundles of rags pretended that they had no idea how the stones had gotten there; a servant, or perhaps a neighbor who had helped, must have done the foul deed. The farmer would wax quite indignant about the carelessness of his help in making "a wrong count" of the bushels of grain. *He*, of course, would never have been so careless.

Storekeepers also considered the customers fair game, and it didn't matter much how prominent a man might be in his community—in trade, almost any sharp practice was considered perfectly legitimate. Barnum later recalled a story that went the rounds in his youth about a grocer who was also a deacon in the church. Before breakfast one morning, the grocer-deacon was overheard calling downstairs to his clerk.

"John, have you watered the rum?"

"Yes, sir."

"And sanded the sugar?"

"Yes, sir."

"And dusted the pepper?"

"Yes, sir."

"And chicoried the coffee?"

"Yes, sir."

"Then come up to prayers."

Such was the moral outlook of rural Connecticut in Barnum's day. Bethel was a strict, highly religious community on Sundays. But on weekdays almost anything went. The life of the people was split into two unequal parts— the intensely practical and the intensely moral. Six days of the week were devoted to the practical, so necessary, as the saying went, to "keep body and soul together"; the seventh day was spent in a stern examination of that soul. No man could travel on horseback or in one of the few carriages before sundown on Sunday unless he was "going to meeting." The stagecoach was not allowed to carry passengers. The stage could roll through Connecticut on its way from New York to Boston because it was carrying the U.S. mail; but a sentinel was posted at each "meeting-house" on its route, and if a passenger had smuggled himself in among the mail bags, the driver and passenger were arrested and held until Monday morning when both would be fined before being allowed to proceed on their way.

In the meetinghouses themselves, the prevailing brand of religion was the sternest Protestantism. Bethel had just one meetinghouse, a Presbyterian one, which all the townspeople, whatever their individual faiths, attended. There was no steeple, no bell, no heat. In the frigid Connecticut winters, women were allowed to bring to church tin boxes filled with live coals to use as footstoves, but the men were expected to endure lengthy sermons, even in zero cold. Though Barnum's grandfather was a Universalist, a relatively gentle brand of religion that Barnum later embraced himself, the boy at this time was under the influence of stern Methodist teachings. Hell always loomed so close that there seemed no possible way for frail human beings to avoid it. Barnum later recalled that, at the age of

13 or 14, after attending one of these meetings "I used to go home and cry and beg God to take me out of existence if He would only save me; but I didn't see much chance for me in the way they put it."

This stern religious creed fitted the pattern of a stern life. Doubtless, the very hardness of the life, the extreme difficulties of the struggle, made it necessary to devote six days to the scrabble for existence and the seventh to an excess of atonement. Virtually everything a family used or ate had to be wrung from the soil or self-created by the hardest kind of daylong labor.

Typical was the never-ending work of the women. The spinning wheel was a fixture in every home, and the women of the family spent long hours spinning their own thread and weaving all the garments for the household. This was only a small part of their daily tasks. They made soap and candles, milked the cows, made butter and cheese, and devoted the rest of their crowded hours to the customary chores of knitting, darning, mending, washing, ironing, and cooking. In such a life, so close to nature, teetering constantly on the edge of want, even water was a precious commodity. Most homes had rain barrels to catch the water pouring off the low, steeply slanted roofs. The rain water was used for washing. Water for drinking and cooking was drawn up from a well in the yard, equipped with an old oaken bucket and a long pole and well sweep. Inside the home, the fireplace furnished the only means of heat, and every effort was made to keep a few live coals overnight by banking up the ashes around them. If, despite this, the coals went out, it was necessary to go to a neighbor the first thing in the morning to collect a live coal with a pair of tongs and bring it back to start the day's fire. Light during the long winter nights was furnished by tallow candles, home made and with dark tow wicks. These were considered so precious that they were hoarded and used most sparingly. In summer it was the custom, except on extraordinary occasions, for the entire family to go to bed at night fall.

Food and eating utensils both were primitive. Plates were almost unknown. In most families, children ate their meals from wooden trenchers. It was considered a sign of prosperity, or extravagance, for a family to discard the trenchers for pewter plates and lead spoons. Food was coarse, but plentiful. There were always plenty of homegrown vegetables, fish that anybody could catch, large clams to be had for the digging, poultry, and meat. The basic dinner, served several times a week, was a meal called pot luck. This consisted of corned beef, salt pork, and vegetables, all boiled together in the huge iron pot that always swung from a crane over the blaze in the great fireplace. Into this pot, along with the meat, would go potatoes, turnips, parsnips, beets, carrots, cabbage, and sometimes onions. On occasion, an Indian pudding, consisting of plain Indian meal mixed with water and kept pretty thick, would be placed in a brown linen bag tied at the top and immersed in the boiling pot luck. When dinner was ready, the Indian pudding would be taken out first, slipped from the bag and eaten with molasses—a dessert that was devoured before the meal.

In Barnum's youth, such was the poverty in Bethel, that

hardly anyone had a wagon or a carriage. Everyone traveled by foot or on horseback. The country doctor visited his patients on horseback, carrying his medicines and instruments in his saddle bags. A wealthy man was a rarity. In later life, Barnum recalled that in his youth the richest man in Bethel was "Esquire Tom Taylor . . . a large, majestic-looking man" who sometimes "wore white-topped boots." Every year Barnum recalled, he took $12 to the squire to pay the interest on a $200 note that his father owed. The squire would get out a small package of notes that he held from persons in the neighborhood; he would leaf through these until he found the note of Barnum's father, and on this he would credit the amount of interest that had been paid. The procedure always fascinated Barnum. How rich Squire Taylor must be! Why, it was rumored in Bethel that he was actually worth all of $3,000! And the rumor, Barnum thought, must be true. For Squire Taylor was so well off that he had actually purchased two yards of figured carpet to put down in front of his bed because the bare board floor was too cold on his feet when he was dressing in winter. This was an extravagance previously unheard of in Bethel. The town agreed that Squire Taylor must be a rich man indeed, but it was inclined to think that he was putting on airs by purchasing that square of carpet for his bedroom.

Such were the times, such the atmosphere in which Barnum was brought up. When even the richest man in the area was thought a spendthrift because he purchased two yards of carpet, it is not difficult to see just how hard the struggle for existence must have been for everyone else. If a fellow was ever going to get ahead and become a rich man like Squire Taylor, worth all of $3,000, he would have to leave no trick unturned, no chance untried. And Phineas Barnum had no intention of missing any chances. He was always keeping an eye out for that extra scheme, that extra income beyond the mere routine of his job.

One of these extra schemes was the lottery. In those days lotteries were the rage of the nation. They were run at the drop of a hat and for almost any purpose—to build a bridge, to establish a school, to support the church. Phineas Taylor, Barnum's grandfather, was the manager of one such lottery, and he instructed his favorite grandson, when the boy was only 12 years old, in the mystery of running such games of chance so that the promoters could always be certain of deriving the greatest benefit. Barnum, thriving on this tutelage, became a lottery salesman and manager, disposing of his tickets among the workmen in the hat and comb factories in nearby Danbury.

What with selling his private stocks of candy, managing the lottery, and clerking in the Bethel store, young Barnum was doing well for a boy not yet 15; but he always, even at this early age, had a sharp eye out "for the main chance," for the novel deal that would lead to the big killing. One day when he was about 14, he felt that he had discovered the magic formula.

A neighbor, John Quigley, had gone up into Litchfield County on a visit. This was about 40 miles from Bethel, a long journey in those times and especially in winter. When Quigley returned and visited the Bethel store, Barnum eagerly questioned him about what he had seen. Had he found anything new or strange in Litchfield?

"Why, yes," Quigley drawled in reply, "I saw something that struck me as being pretty curious. I saw a dog of ordinary size that had two natural tails, one about three feet long."

Barnum became excited at once.

"That is really a curiosity!" he exclaimed.

He began to go through some rapid mental gymnastics. If he could get possession of this freak dog, if he could bring the animal back to Bethel and put him on exhibition, he could charge admission from people who would be eager to see such a strange sight. Why, he could make a small fortune!

"Do you suppose I could buy him?" he asked Quigley.

"Why, yes," Quigley replied slowly, "I guess that five or ten dollars would buy him."

Barnum, now running a fever envisioning the fortune that could be made out of the dog with two tails, began to make plans at once to leave for Litchfield in the morning. Quigley, after discussing the matter with him for some time, finally prepared to go home. As he departed, he said over his shoulder:

"Better see me in the morning before you go. I might thing of something that would help you."

The next morning was bitter cold, but Barnum was not to be discouraged. He put on thick boots, a big overcoat, a heavy muffler, and a knitted wool cap; he mounted one of his father's horses; and he set out for Litchfield. On the way, he stopped at Quigley's home to see if his friend had thought of any new angle that might help him in his negotiations for the dog with two tails.

[29]

"Well, John," he said to Quigley, "I'm off to Litchfield. I'm going to get that dog somehow or other. Have you any suggestions?"

Quigley nodded slowly.

"Matter of fact, I have," he said. "There's one thing I forget to mention. That dog with two tails was coming out of a tanyard when I saw him, and one of the tails was a cow's tail that he carried in his mouth!"

The whole yarn, like the story of the Ivy Island inheritance, had been one of those practical jokes in which the people of the day so delighted because they relieved the monotony and the drudgery of a hard existence. Once more Barnum was the butt of village wisecracks. Everyone kept asking him with the straightest and most innocent of faces if he had yet found "the dog with two tails." Barnum bore up well under the joshing. As the saying goes, "He laughs best who laughs last," and Barnum, at 14, had had a swift-flashing idea for profit—the very kind of an idea that, in not too many years, was to make him world-renowned as the Prince of Showmen.

Chapter **3**

He Learns to Advertise

Wen Barnum was 15 years old, his life suddenly was overshadowed by tragedy. In March, 1825, his father was taken ill with a severe attack of fever. He never recovered, but grew steadily weaker. On Sept. 7, 1825, he died at the age of 48. Barnum, standing by his bedside, felt nakedly alone in the world, utterly forlorn. And, as he soon discovered, he was penniless.

He had lent his father all the extra money he had made by selling lottery tickets and from various other schemes. His father had given him a note for the amount. But the administrators of the estate quickly decided that, since Barnum was a minor, he had no claim because everything he possessed really had belonged to his father anyhow. Barnum was left without a cent to his name, so poor that he had to clerk in a Bethel store to "work out" the cost of the new pair of shoes that he wore to his father's funeral.

"I can truly say, therefore," he later wrote, "that I

began the world with nothing, and was barefooted at that."

The death of Philo Barnum left his entire family impoverished. Barnum's father had never really succeeded at anything; and when he died, he had twice as many debts as assets. Barnum's mother was left with her five children, no money, and no visible means of supporting herself or them. Barnum, the oldest, already had demonstrated that he was self-sufficient, but the smaller children, the youngest only seven, were not much help. A courageous, hardworking woman, Mrs. Barnum decided to continue to run the village tavern. She was so industrious, she pinched pennies so successfully, that within a few years she had worked herself out of debt and had cleared the family homestead. In the meantime, Barnum, having worked out the price of his funeral shoes, began to hunt for a position that offered a better opportunity than clerking for his father's partner in the Bethel store.

He found the job he was looking for in Grassy Plain, a mile northwest of Bethel. There James S. Keeler and Lewis Whitlock ran a general store, and Barnum went to work for them. His wages were a munificent $6 a month and board. His mother did his washing. Keeler and Whitlock, however, permitted Barnum to run some speculations of his own on the side; and by hard work and saving, he soon managed to get "a little sum of money ahead." His new employers soon discovered that he was a sharp trader, and they often left him in sole charge of the store. This practice resulted in what seemed a harebrained trade on Barnum's part.

One day when he was alone in the store, a peddler came

along with a large wagon filled with glass bottles of all sizes, ranging from a half-pint to a gallon. The peddler, figuring the young clerk for an easy mark, tried to sell him some of the bottles—and was astounded when Barnum blandly offered to dicker for the entire load!

Barnum astonished the peddler by buying the whole wagonload.

There was much haggling about the price, but Barnum, as he later wrote, "managed to pay him off in unsaleable goods at exorbitant prices." When Keeler returned to the store shortly afterwards, he was stunned to find the place literally overrun with empty bottles.

"What under heavens have you been doing?" he asked.

"I have been trading goods for bottles," Barnum said.

"You have made a fool of yourself," Keeler exclaimed, "for you have enough bottles to supply the whole town for 20 years."

"Don't be alarmed," Barnum told him. "I'll get rid of the lot within three months."

"If you can do that," Keeler said, "you can perform a miracle."

Barnum set himself to the task. His problem was to find a way to dispose of a wagonload of virtually worthless, empty glass bottles at a handsome profit. This, at first glance, seemed an impossibility, but Barnum had had an idea in the back of his mind when he traded for the bottles.

He had already discovered that the Grassy Plains general store was cluttered with a large amount of old, unsaleable merchandise. It was overloaded especially with battered, tarnished, and dirty tinware that no one wanted; Keeler and Whitlock had written off the accumulation in their minds as one of the unavoidable losses that result from business. Barnum, however, had the notion that this worthless old stock could be disposed of at a profit.

What he decided to do was to run a lottery. On rainy days, when business was slow, he devoted several hours to perfecting his scheme. He would offer a great number of prizes to delude the public into the belief that they almost certainly could get something for nothing. His top prize would be $25, consisting of any merchandise in the store the winner wanted. This made a fine lure. And Barnum backed this up by offering 550 smaller prizes, 50 of them for $5 each. The catch was that the winners of the smaller prizes couldn't pick and choose what they wanted. The store would designate what they must take. And the store had a tremendous amount of battered tinware and empty glass bottles to get rid of!

This fascinating aspect of the lottery was well concealed in the glowing blurb which Barnum drew up. In the most extravagant terms, he billed his self-promoted lottery as the most certain gamble of a lifetime. The lottery ticket holder almost couldn't miss. Barnum's poster fairly screamed the good news. "MAGNIFICENT LOTTERY! $25 FOR ONLY 50 CTS. OVER 550 PRIZES!!! ONLY 1000 TICKETS!!!! GOODS PUT IN AT THE LOWEST CASH PRICES!!!!!"

The appeal to human greed was irresistible. The tickets, Barnum wrote, "went like wildfire," especially since the "customers did not stop to consider the nature of the prizes." All of the tickets were quickly sold, reaping a cash harvest of $500 that represented a veritable windfall in that day. The whole countryside waited with impatience for the day of the great drawing. At the appointed hour, Barnum drew out the winning 550 tickets. Then, and only then, came disillusionment.

A man who had bought 20 tickets and had drawn 10 winners found that his "prizes" consisted entirely of empty glass bottles. Barnum's own uncle, Aaron Nichols, a hat manufacturer, had bought twelve tickets, and seven had been winners. "Unfortunately," Barnum later wrote, "they were all to be paid in *tin!* He took them home one day in his wagon—looking like a tin peddler as he went through the street." Barnum's aunt was furious, especially when she discovered that no amount of scrubbing would clean up the dirty, tarnished tinware. To get even, she baked Barnum the nicest pie, wrapped it beautifully, and sent it to him—in one of the dirty, tin pie plates that she hadn't even tried to scrub!

Within ten days, all of the battered old tinware and all of the empty glass bottles had disappeared from the Grassy Plain store. Naturally, Barnum's employers, who had seen him turn worthless goods into real money, were delighted by his performance. Just as naturally, the prize-winners who had lugged out bushel baskets full of worthless tin and glass bottles were peeved at having been so outrageously taken. "Some of the customers were vexed," Barnum later acknowledged, certainly the mildest of under-statements, but so many ticket holders were in the same fix, so many had been duped, that eventually they began to laugh at each other and the whole thing passed off as a joke —a colossal hoax that marked young P. T. Barnum as a smart one.

While Barnum was clerking at the Grassy Plain store, he boarded during the week with Mrs. Jerusha Wheeler, whom everyone knew as "Aunt Rushia." On Saturday nights, he would get a horse and ride into Bethel to spend Sunday with his mother. This simple routine led directly to what, for Barnum, was an exciting development. One Saturday evening in summer, a series of violent thunderstorms swept over the Connecticut valleys. The proprietor of a millinery shop across the street from the general store sent word to Barnum that a young girl from Bethel had ridden up on horseback to get her new bonnet, but she was afraid to go back alone in the stormy night. When Barnum was ready to go to Bethel, would he call at the milliner's shop and escort the young girl home?

Barnum agreed, and so it was that he met Charity Hallett, a fair, rosy-cheeked girl with beautiful white teeth. Before they had finished the mile ride to Bethel in the lightning-lit night, Barnum was smitten with a new and strange ailment: he was in love. He learned that Charity Hallett worked for a tailor in Bethel. The next day, at church, he saw her again from a distance and found her every bit as beautiful in the daylight as she had appeared in the stormy night. Every Sunday during the rest of that summer he returned to Bethel, went to church, and gazed upon Charity Hallett. But, with the timidity of the extremely young in love, he found "no opportunity . . . to renew the acquaintance."

That autumn Barnum began to look for a better opportunity. It was obvious to him that the Grassy Plain store offered no future. Despite his success with the famous bottle lottery, his employers had seen no reason to raise his wages. As a result, he was ready to move on. When a Danbury man who had opened a grocery store in Brooklyn, offered him a job there, Barnum promptly took it. Soon he was placed in full charge of the store; and in the capacity of store manager, he learned the technique of bargain hunting in New York, seeking always the dealers from whom goods might be obtained at "the lowest cash price" and the auctions at which he might find a bargain in tea, sugar, and other groceries.

[37]

Barnum was prospering when, in the summer of 1827, he was stricken with smallpox. For weeks he lay desperately ill in a rooming house, alone and friendless in a strange city. When he finally recovered, he staggered to a pier and booked passage on a boat going up Long Island Sound to Bethel. There, at his mother's tavern, he spent a month recuperating; chatting with old friends and acquaintances; and, in his own words, finding "several opportunities of slightly renewing the short acquaintance" with that charming tailor's helper, Charity Hallett. At the end of the month, his funds exhausted, Barnum tore himself away from Bethel and Charity, and returned to his job in the Brooklyn grocery store. He stayed only a short time before establishing his own "porter-house," or bar, in New York. Within a few months, he sold out this business at a slight profit and went to work in a larger porter-house much frequented by visiting Danbury and Bethel combmakers. Here he renewed old acquaintances, heard the news from home, and often took Connecticut friends out upon the town, showing them the sights of New York and attending the theater. He was having a good time, but making no appreciable progress when, in February, 1828, he received a letter from his grandfather, Phineas Taylor.

The old man wanted his favorite grandson to come back to Bethel and settle down. The grandfather owned a carriage house on the main street of the village, and he offered Barnum the use of a portion of it, rent free, if he would return and set up some kind of business. Barnum's capital was not large, only $120, but he decided to plunge it all on the venture. He spent $50 fixing up a store and, with the balance, laid in a stock of fruits and confectioneries bought from dealers with whom he had become acquainted while working in New York.

The day that Barnum picked for his grand opening was one that had happy associations for him—the first Monday of May, military training day in Bethel. Perhaps recalling his boyhood success with cherry rum, he included among the stock of his new store a barrel of ale. Barnum was haunted by the fear rain might reduce the crowds that always flocked to the village to witness the drill; but the day dawned fine and clear, and before noon he was so busy waiting on customers that he had to summon an old school friend to help him out. At the end of training day the barrel of ale had been emptied, and so many of Barnum's cakes, candies, nuts and raisins had been sold that he counted up $63 for his day's receipts. And he still had a good part of his stock left. His store was a success.

Enterprising as always, he invested his profits in additional stock. Perhaps the memory of the New York toy shop that had lured him to his boyhood downfall stuck in his mind, for he laid in a similar assortment of novelties, pocketbooks, beads, finger rings, combs, knives, and toys. In the fall, he put up a big sign proclaiming that, in addition to his other wares, he was offering fresh-made oyster stew. Business boomed, but Barnum was never one to be content with just a little boom—he must always seek a bigger. And so, following his grandfather's sage advice, he got himself appointed agent for a large lottery and began to sell lottery tickets on commission.

His store became a center for visitors and town gossip.

One of his regular visitors was a man of wealth, a personage who had achieved this admirable status by the kind of showmanship that was not lost on Barnum. The rich man's name was Hackariah Bailey, known to everyone as "Hack." He found a simple road to fortune. He had imported the first elephant ever brought to the United States, and so great was the people's curiosity, so eager were they to see this strange animal, that Hack Bailey had reaped a golden harvest by exhibiting his elephant all over the nation. With his elephant profits, he went into the steamboat business and became a successful operator of excursion boats traveling up the Hudson River. With the profits from the elephant and the steamboats, he then built a fine hotel at Somers, N. Y. In tribute to the source of his good fortune, he called it the Elephant Hotel. In front of it he erected a large stone pillar crowned by a golden elephant. Hack Bailey's success was graphic proof that a man might amass huge riches if he could only find an attraction novel enough to excite the curiosity of the American people.

The lesson was not lost on Barnum, though at the moment two far more important matters claimed the major part of his attention. One was Charity Hallett; the other, the lottery. Barnum had recovered from his bashfulness where "the fair tailoress" was concerned. He associated with all the young people and attended their parties, picnics, and sleigh rides; but Charity "continued to stand highest in [his] estimation and to improve upon acquaintance." Grandfather Taylor had a kindly hand in furthering the romance. He owned a number of horses and vehicles, and a horse and conveyance of some kind were always at the disposal of his favorite grandson. There were just two exceptions. Grandfather Taylor had a favorite horse, which he called "the Arabian," and a new sleigh, the finest in the village. These he would not let Barnum have. And these, naturally, Barnum wanted.

He knew that with such a turnout he could eclipse all the other young men in the village; and so he decided to break his grandfather's fixed rule. There was, he told Phineas Taylor, a sleighing party set for the next Tuesday, and he would need a horse and sleigh. "All right," his grandfather said.

"Can I have the Arabian and the new sleigh?" Barnum asked.

His grandfather, surprised by the request, snapped without thinking:

"Yes, if you have $20 in your pocket!"

Barnum whipped out his wallet, showed his grandfather that it contained $20, then pocketed it again.

"There, you see I have the $20," he said smoothly. "I am obliged to you. I suppose I can have the Arab and the new sleigh?"

Phineas Taylor had meant, of course, that Barnum should pay him $20 if he took the favorite horse and sleigh. But this wasn't what he had said, and he chuckled at the swiftness with which his grandson had turned the tables on him.

"Yes, you may have them, but use them carefully," he told Barnum.

Barnum promised, and he and Charity were the most splendidly turned-out young couple at that sleigh ride.

[*41*]

The second great interest of Barnum's life at this period prospered just as did his romance. Lotteries were then legal in Connecticut; and gambling on lottery tickets was a fever, a disease, that swept the entire countryside. "Thousands of persons are at this day squandering in lottery tickets and lottery policies the monies which their families need," Barnum wrote later—when he was no longer involved personally in the business! The managers of the lotteries, by one device or another, always took out for themselves more than 57 cents of every dollar played, leaving less than 43 cents to be divided among the players in prizes. This meant, of course, that in the long run the players as a class would be impoverished and only the manipulators of the lotteries would profit. Still the possibility, however unlikely, of obtaining a big cash prize for a small risk lured the gullible to participate in a daily gamble they could ill afford. Barnum could moralize about this later, but at the moment he took full advantage of the popular fever.

He plastered the walls of his store with gaudily printed handbills and circulars. "Immense gold signs, and placards in inks and papers of all colors covered my lottery office," he later wrote. He distributed handbills by the thousands across the Connecticut countryside. Every time one of his players won—and with thousands playing somebody occasionally *had* to win—a new handbill advertised the fact in terms designed to make each individual player believe that, almost certainly, he would win tomorrow. By such devices, Barnum expanded his lottery business to the point where he had an office in Danbury and agents in all the country towns roundabout; he was selling from $500 to $2,000 worth of tickets a day, a fantastic figure considering the tight money values of the time.

Barnum, at 19, was rapidly becoming a man of wealth, and he began to consider setting up a household of his own. His mother and some of his other relations evidently considered that he was looking beneath him in casting his eyes in the direction of Charity Hallett, but for Barnum there was no one quite like "the fair tailoress." In the summer of 1829, he proposed and Charity accepted him. In October, she went to New York, pretending that she was going to visit her uncle. Shortly afterwards, Barnum went to New York, pretending that he was going to buy goods for his store. With no one in Bethel having any suspicion of what was about to happen, the two pretenders met in the home of Charity's uncle; and there, on November 7, 1829, they were married.

Life was certainly smiling on P. T. Barnum. In June, 1830, he bought three acres of land near Bethel from his grandfather and erected a two-and-a-half story house for himself and his bride. In the spring of 1831, he built what came to be known in Bethel as "the yellow store." He stocked this with everything from dry goods to hardware, the varied and all-inclusive stock of the general country store of that day. It looked almost as if everything that Barnum touched would succeed, but just at this point, as so often happens when everything is going most smoothly, trouble came to Barnum.

All New England in 1831 became possessed by a religious frenzy. Daylong religious meetings were held;

those attending were verbally whipped and exhorted into an excess of passion and fanaticism; suicides—and sometimes murders—resulted. Even this was not all. Zealots among the ministers proposed that a Christian Party be formed in politics and that none except "professors of religion" should be allowed to hold public office. Barnum, who was a Democrat like his grandfather, was horrified by these excesses and alarmed for the future of the country if such religious madmen were to assume full control of its destiny.

Aroused by this prospect, Barnum took up his pen and wrote a number of articles opposing the religious fanaticism around him and exposing its dangers to democracy. These articles he sent to the editor of the nearest weekly newspaper in Danbury. The editor, like many another before and since, evidently hesitated to cause trouble for himself by opposing what appeared to be the prevailing mood in his district. So, although he printed other letters on less controversial subjects, he just couldn't find room for Barnum's offerings. Convinced by this conspiracy of silence that the term "free press" was a myth, Barnum took action. He purchased type and a printing press, and began to publish in Danbury his own weekly newspaper, the *Herald of Freedom*.

With vigor and boldness, Barnum lashed out at the prevailing frenzy of the times. He was controversial; he was exciting; and soon the public, intrigued to learn whom he might attack next, was buying the *Herald*. It was not long before, in Barnum's words, the paper commanded "a liberal circulation, not only in the vicinity of its publication, but large numbers of copies were sent into nearly every State in the Union."

Such notoriety, such outspokenness carries with it its own dangers. Soon Barnum was sued for libel by a Danbury butcher whom he had accused of acting as a spy at a Democratic caucus. The butcher collected several hundred dollars damages. Still Barnum was not daunted. He next accused a deacon of "taking usury of an orphan boy." If he had used any other term, it might not have been so bad. He could have accused the deacon of extortion, or imposing outrageous charges on the orphan boy; but usury—this was a crime denounced in the Bible. The deacon sued, and the judge, a strong churchman himself, charged the jury so vigorously that he left it with no doubt where its duty lay. The jury saw the light and convicted Barnum, and the judge sentenced the brash, 21-year-old editor to pay a fine of $100 and spend 60 days in jail.

Never did a court verdict more quickly make a hero of the victim. Barnum certainly had made himself heartily disliked among the cautious officialdom of his time, a fate that can be almost guaranteed for any crusading editor; but he had struck a responsive chord among the public who were attracted by his courage and candor. When he was sentenced, the public felt he had been punished for championing their own interests, and sentiment switched heavily to his side. His cell in the Danbury jail was papered and carpeted. Friends visited him at will. In effect, Barnum turned his cell into an office, and from it he continued to edit the *Herald of Freedom*. Hundreds of new subscriptions poured in. The two months in prison were two months not so much of punishment as of new success. When the day came that Barnum was to be freed, his friends and indignant defenders of a free press combined to give him a celebration that rocked the countryside.

In the very courtroom where he had been sentenced, a large crowd gathered. An ode, especially written for the occasion, was recited; an oration, "The Freedom of the Press," was delivered. Then several hundred guests sat down to "a sumptuous repast," spiced by speeches and toasts that continued throughout the afternoon. At the end of the day, Barnum was escorted from the scene of celebration and seated in a coach drawn by six horses. A cavalcade of forty horsemen carrying the United States flag preceded him. A band played patriotic tunes loudly. Behind the coach came 60 carriages bearing the happy celebrants from Barnum's party. For three miles across the Connecticut countryside from Danbury to Bethel, the procession wound its way. Arriving at last in front of Barnum's house, the band struck up "Home, Sweet Home"! The crowd gave three lusty cheers; then, with flags still waving, band still blaring, the Barnum partisans paraded back to Danbury.

This triumph may be said to have marked the high point of Barnum's career in Bethel. The unvarying success he had enjoyed now suddenly gave out. He had bought recklessly and not too wisely for "the yellow store"; in an effort to do a greater volume of business, he had extended credit to many who either could not or would not pay. His ledger contained acid entries showing how these accounts were "balanced" to Barnum's disadvantage. "By death, to balance," read one entry. "By running away, in full," was another. "By cheating me out of my dues, to balance," was a third. In disgust, Barnum finally sold the store.

Hardly had he done so when he suffered another blow. The Connecticut legislature passed a law banning lotteries and thus at one stroke abolished the most profitable business Barnum had. Only the *Herald of Freedom* was left, and this was not making money. The religious frenzy that had called it into being had subsided; hard New England common sense had reasserted itself. With the death of controversy, subscriptions fell off. Barnum could see no future in the *Herald,* and so, in the fall of 1834, having brought out 160 issues of the paper, he turned it over to his brother-in-law and retired from the publishing business.

Having disposed of his general store, having been legislated out of the lottery business, having abandoned his career as an editor, Barnum had nothing left in Bethel to occupy him or to promise a future. He was only 24, and doubtless he could have established himself in some other line of business. But Bethel had begun to seem too small and too cramped for his tastes. He look off across the Connecticut hills "to York," the magical city of his boyhood, the city whose busy tempo had drawn him as a youth. He decided to go there, and to gamble on the future.

As winter closed in, he sold his house. He gathered together what little money he had left; turned the accounts due him over to an agent to collect if he could; and with his wife, Charity, and his infant daughter, Caroline, he left for the great city, determined to hunt there the path to fortune.

Chapter 4

The First Marvel

The New York to which Barnum brought his family was a half-formed city of some 200,000 persons. It was gay, bustling, crude. Broadway was only four miles long and ended in a country lane. Washington Square, now in "lower" Manhattan, was considered quite a long distance north of the city proper. Half-grown as it was, New York was already the hub of commerce and of wealth. Homes were more imposing and better furnished than elsewhere in the United States; the shop catered to expensive tastes; the theater and allied entertainment lines represented a big industry. Indicative of the well-off state of the city's upper classes was the number of gigs, phaetons and coaches of all kinds that cluttered its streets. For the poorer citizens, a newfangled horsecar line clattered its way on a single track up one of the city's streets. And when one crossed Broadway, one had to look out for the pigs that waddled along in the wake of the passing carriages, hunting cast-off morsels of food.

In this strange, hurrying, gay and still rough city, Barnum rented a house for his family on Hudson Street and set out to look for work. He had hoped to find, not just a job, but some kind of position in which he could exchange his skills for a share in the profits of the enterprise. But he quickly found that New Yorkers were hard men to convince that sharing profits was to their advantage. Daily he studied the want ads in the *Sun;* daily he trudged the streets running down what appeared to be alluring prospects; and each night he returned home tired, empty-handed, discouraged. As he quickly learned, most of the advertisers were looking for some gullible soul who could be easily separated from his money. Schemers trying to promote some pet idea would offer Barnum a share of the profits, provided he put up all the money to get the scheme going. Barnum was offered a share of the fortune to be made from marketing new miracle-working pills, marvelous mouse traps, and a thing called a "hydro-oxygen microscope." Promoters of such ventures invariably wanted several hundred dollars of Barnum's money; and Barnum, even if he had been interested, simply didn't have that kind of money to invest.

In desperation, to help meet the immediate needs of his family, he finally got himself a job as a "drummer," or commission agent, for a cap store. At this he worked until the spring of 1835. Then his agent in Bethel sent him several hundred dollars he had been able to collect from persons who had owned Barnum for everything from groceries to lottery tickets. With this capital, Barnum and his wife promptly opened a private boardinghouse at 52

Frankfort Street, near Franklin Square, then the business center of the town. The house was also close to the docks where passengers from Connecticut landed. Barnum advertised his new boardinghouse in the Connecticut newspapers; and since country people visiting the strange city liked to stop with someone they knew, he was soon doing a thriving business. The profits were so good in fact, that he was able to purchase a half-interest in a neighborhood grocery store run by John Moody at 156 South Street.

Such was the situation, such were Barnum's suddenly brighter prospects when in July, 1835, a friend from Connecticut who knew both Barnum and Moody entered the South Street grocery with a piece of information that was to change Barnum's entire life.

The visitor was a man named Coley Bartram, of Redding. While talking to Barnum, he happened to mention that he recently had been part owner of an extraordinary Negro woman who was believed to be 161 years old and to have been the nurse of George Washington. Bartram said he had sold out his interest in the woman, Joice Heth, to his partner, R. W. Lindsay, of Jefferson County, Ky. Lindsay was still exhibiting this human phenomenon in Philadelphia, Bartram said; but Lindsay didn't have much skill as a showman, he was not succeeding very well, and he was eager to sell Joice Heth and return to his home in Kentucky.

As proof that he was not just spinning a tall tale, Bartram showed Barnum an advertisement that had appeared in the *Pennsylvania Inquirer* of July 15, 1835. This proclaimed that Joice Heth had been born near the Potomac River and had been a member of the Baptist Church for 116 years. After nursing George Washington, she had been sold; her new owners, "the Bowling family," had taken her to Kentucky, where she had lived for some 90 years. Lindsay claimed that he had "the original bill of sale of Augustine Washington [George's father], in his own handwriting" and that this and other evidence would "satisfy even the most incredulous."

Barnum, who at 14 had set out to ride across the winterbound Connecticut countryside in pursuit of "the dog with two tails"; Barnum, who had had a vivid first-hand lesson from Hack Bailey of the fortune to be made by exhibiting an elephant; Barnum, who had always kept his eye out "for the main chance," and had long been convinced that a fortune could be made from exhibiting the right kind of curiosity—this Barnum, leagues removed from the shopkeeper Barnum, was instantly excited by the prospect. He sniffed a possible fortune in Joice Heth if she was all that Bartram swore she was. In a great fever of impatience, Barnum set out for Philadelphia.

He went at once to the exhibition hall, had an interview with Lindsay and saw Joice Heth. There could be no doubt that she was old—so old that, as Barnum said, "she might almost as well have been called a thousand years old as any other age." She was lying on a lounge in the middle of the room, an almost complete cripple. Her legs, drawn up and bent at the knees, were so rigid they could not be straightened. She had the free use of her right arm, but the left arm was paralyzed and lay clasped across her breast. She was blind and she had no teeth; her thick, bushy,

[52]

gray hair made her appear almost like some strange monstrosity from the African jungles. The nails on the fingers of her useless left hand were four inches long; because the fingers had been drawn inward and downward by the paralysis, the long, talon-like nails extended above her wrist.

Joice Heth looked the part of a wrinkled crone, a creature of inhuman antiquity, but she was, as Barnum soon discovered, mentally alert and volubly sociable. She would talk in a steady stream as long as a visitor would stay and converse with her. She sang a number of ancient hymns, so old they had fallen into disuse and been forgotten; and she talked almost endlessly about her "dear little George." She declared to Barnum that she had been present at the birth of the future father of his country and that she was the first person to put clothes upon him. "In fact," said Joice—and it was a favorite expression of hers—"I raised him."

Barnum was greatly impressed by this exhibition, and his agile mind began to teem with plans to turn Joice Heth's performance into profit. But he was cautious. He asked Lindsay for the positive proof he had said he had that Joice Heth was indeed 161 years old and the nurse of George Washington. Lindsay produced a wrinkled document that, in its own way, looked old and tattered enough to fit the supposed age of Joice Heth. It was a bill of sale dated February 5, 1727 by which Augustine Washington deeded to his sister-in-law and neighbor, Elizabeth Atwood, "one negro woman, named Joice Heth, aged fifty-four years, for and in consideration of the sum of thirty-three pounds lawful money of Virginia." Joice explained that her husband had been the slave of Mrs. Atwood, and for that reason

[53]

the sale had been made. As the Atwoods and Washingtons were neighbors, however, she was nearby five years later when George was born. Because she had previously been the Washington family nurse, she was called in to help.

"The story seemed plausible," Barnum later wrote—and plausible was enough for Barnum; plausible was all that Barnum needed. Truth might be something else; but Barnum could make a fortune out of that "plausible" story of Joice Heth's, provided only that it would hold together well enough so that no one could shoot holes in it. There was, of course, one question that almost everybody would ask, and Barnum had to satisfy himself about what the answer would be. The question: How did it happen that a woman with such famous past associations had gone so long undiscovered?

Well, Lindsay said, she had been sold by the Atwoods to the Bowling family and had gone off with them to Kentucky. She had lived on the Bowling estate for so many years that no one in the family remembered anything about her past. To the modern generation of Bowlings, Joice Heth had been just another old and crippled woman, living in an outlying building on the estate. By the purest chance, said Lindsay, one of the Bowlings, searching for old bills of sale in the Virginia record office, had come across the ancient deed from Augustine Washington. Then, for the first time, the Bowlings realized that they had in Joice Heth a valuable piece of human property.

Barnum naturally wanted to know just how valuable Lindsay considered "the property" now. Lindsay guessed Joice Heth should be worth all of $3,000; but Barnum, the expert from boyhood in "lowest cash price" deals, soon worked the price down to $1,000, provided it was paid in ten days. Barnum at the moment did not have $1,000; he had only $500 cash. But he was determined to buy Joice Heth, and so he hurried back to New York, sold out his half-interest in the grocery to his partner, Moody, and raised the necessary money. Returning to Philadelphia, Barnum paid Lindsay. Now that he owned Joice Heth, Barnum had to decide how he was to make a fortune exhibiting her. Time was needed for planning, for strategy, and Lindsay agreed to continue with his Philadelphia exhibition to give Barnum a chance to make New York properly appreciative of the great treat that was in store for it.

Barnum, the born promoter, now went to work on his first great promotion. In New York he made a deal with William Niblo, owner of Niblo's Garden, one of the most famous saloons and gathering-places of its day. Niblo owned a dwelling house near his saloon, and he agreed to let Barnum have a large apartment in it to stage the exhibition of Joice Heth. Niblo would furnish the lights, pay the expense of printing and advertising, and provide a ticket-seller. For these services, he was to receive one-half of the gross receipts.

Having acquired an exhibition hall, Barnum went to work to make the entire public of New York Joice Heth-conscious. He engaged Levi Lyman, a charming but lazy lawyer from Penn Yan, N. Y., to help him handle the exhibition chores. Lyman wrote a brief memoir of Joice, illustrated with her portrait, which he put in pamphlet form

[55]

for sale to visitors at six cents a copy. Barnum used the same portrait on innumerable handbills and huge posters with which he practically blanketed the city. In these, he proclaimed that "Joice Heth is unquestionably the most astonishing and interesting curiosity in the world." After describing Joice's role in practically "raising" George Washington, Barnum informed New Yorkers: "She is cheerful and healthy, although she weighs but forty-five pounds. She relates many anecdotes of her young master; she speaks also of the red-coats during the Revolutionary War, but does not appear to hold them in high estimation." Crowds in other cities had visited Joice Heth, Barnum told New Yorkers: she had been examined by "many clergymen and physicians, who have pronounced her the most ancient specimen of mortality the oldest of them has ever seen or heard of. . . ."

With such expert advance press-agentry, Joice Heth came to New York and practically took the city by storm. The *Sun* reported that "this renowned relic of the olden time has created quite a sensation among the lovers of the curious and the marvellous; and a greater object of marvel and curiosity has never presented itself for their gratification." Crowds came to see Joice Heth, and soon Barnum was pulling in gross receipts of $1,500 a week, a huge take in that day. For weeks, New Yorkers flocked to see this ancient slave woman, asking her questions about the Washington family, listening enthralled to her tales about "dear little George," entranced by the almost forgotten hymns she sang in her cracked, reedy voice.

When New Yorkers' curiosity about Joice began to

wear thin, Barnum took his ancient property on tour. In Providence and Boston, he drew big crowds. This was Barnum's first visit to Boston, and there he met a veteran showman named Maelzel. Maelzel predicted that Barnum would succeed in show business, for, he said, "you understand the value of the press, and that is the great thing. Nothing helps showmans like the types and the ink."

Barnum bombarded Boston with a steady stream of publicity about Joice Heth; and when Boston audiences began to fall off, he pulled a new trick out of his hat. He sent a letter to a Boston newspaper, signed only "A Visitor." The letter charged that Joice Heth was a complete fraud— she wasn't even a living human being. She was nothing more than a dummy made of India rubber, whalebone and hidden springs, and her exhibitor was a skilled ventriloquist.

This denunciation promptly whipped up a heated controversy, a development that made Barnum sit back and rub his hands with glee. For only one man stood to benefit from such controversy—Barnum. Those who had already seen Joice Heth and had accepted her for what she appeared to be wanted to come back and see her again to decide for themselves whether it was possible they had been deceived. And those who hadn't seen her were lured into coming to try to decide for themselves the riddle Barnum had posed: Was she an incredibly ancient human being or a preposterous, animated rubber doll? With this kind of stimulus, Barnum and Joice Heth had a long and profitable run in Boston.

When the curiosity of Bostonians finally had been exhausted, Barnum took Joice on tour through such New England cities as Lowell, Worcester, Springfield, and Hartford. A return engagement at Niblo's Garden in New York followed; and after this, Barnum and the ancient slave tapped the pocketbooks of curious crowds in New Haven, Newark, Albany and other cities.

Barnum, without a doubt, had found his true vocation, but it was a precarious one. His one attraction was Joice Heth; and Joice, whether she was 161 years old or not, was so old that it was obvious she could not be expected to live forever. Nor did she. She became ill during a second exhibition in Boston and was taken, with a Negro woman to attend her, to the home of Barnum's brother, Philo, in Bethel. There she died on February 19, 1836, and Philo Barnum shipped her body by sleigh to Barnum in New York for whatever disposition he might choose to make of it.

This simple act resulted in the final sensation in the brief, gaudy career of Joice Heth, human phenomenon. Barnum recalled that an eminent New York surgeon, while witnessing Joice Heth's act in Niblo's, had expressed a desire to conduct a postmortem examination of her body in the hope of determining her true age. Barnum had agreed. And so now, with Joice dead, the physician reminded Barnum of his promise; and Barnum, keeping it, arranged for the last, macabre exhibition of the woman who had thrilled audiences with the tale of how she had cuddled the newborn "dear little George."

A large audience gathered for the dissection—and the verdict. Physicians, students, clergymen, editors—all were present during the postmortem. The result was disastrous to the myth from which Barnum had been reaping a small fortune. The arteries around the heart of the dead Joice Heth were in such good condition that the examining expert informed Barnum gravely that Joice could not have been 161 years old; indeed, he doubted if she was over 80. Barnum protested that he had "hired" Joice in perfect good faith, that he had relied upon her appearance and the documents the Kentuckian, Lindsay, had furnished him as proof of her great age. So began a new controversy that was, perversely, not to damage Barnum, but to enhance his reputation.

The *Sun*, in an article describing the autopsy, declared that it had exposed "one of the most precious humbugs that ever was imposed upon a credulous community." But, oddly enough, few New Yorkers would credit the truth. Those who had seen Joice Heth with their own eyes preferred to believe that she had really been as old as they thought she had been.

"There must be some mistake," said one, "for her very appearance indicated she must have been at least 120."

"She could not have been less than 100," said another.

This popular clinging to the myth of Joice Heth inspired Levi Lyman, Barnum's partner, to embark upon a series of practical jokes that were to have far-reaching consequences. Lyman went to James Gordon Bennett, one of the most famous newspapermen of the time and editor of the *Herald*. Bennett's paper and the *Sun* were rivals; and so Lyman told Bennett exactly what Bennett was delighted to hear—that what had really happened was that the *Sun* had been duped, had been made the victim of a hoax. Joice Heth was still alive and still doing her exhibitions in Connecticut, Lyman solemnly assured Bennett; what had happened was that Barnum had fooled everybody by substituting for Joice's body the body of a Harlem Negress. With a whoop of joy, Bennett leaped upon the story and ran a long front page story of the way in which the *Sun* had been hoodwinked.

There followed what, from Barnum's standpoint, was the most delightful of newspaper wars. The *Sun* indignantly shouted back it *had not* been hoodwinked. The physician who had examined Joice shouted indignantly that he *had not* been hoodwinked. Bennett continued to roar mightily at both of them that they had. But as time passed and no Joice Heth appeared in exhibition halls anywhere, it began to dawn upon Bennett that *he* had been made the victim of the real hoax. He seethed with fury. In September, 1836, chancing to meet Lyman upon the street, Bennett exploded in rage. Lyman took the public dressing down—and laughed. It had been just an innocent little joke, he said; now, if Bennett would only listen to him, he would make amends, he would tell the editor the *real* story about Joice Heth.

Lyman must have been an extremely persuasive talker; for, though Bennett knew he had been gulled once, he couldn't resist the new story that Lyman fed him. This was that Barnum had created the whole Joice Heth fraud. Barnum had found the old woman, Lyman said; he had had all her teeth extracted, he had taught her the ancient hymns, he had invented the entire story that she had been George Washington's nurse, and he had drilled her to tell it so convincingly all America had been hoodwinked. It was a preposterous story, one which all the evidence indicated hadn't a word of truth in it; but Bennett, with another whoop of joy at proving himself so much wiser than his competitors, printed it all at great length under the headline, "The Joice Heth Hoax!"

This time, Bennett was believed. New Yorkers accepted his detailed account of the manner in which Barnum had made up the whole Joice Heth legend as the real truth of the matter. They were helped to this belief by Barnum himself. He uttered no word of denial. For 20 years, until he wrote his autobiography, he let everybody believe that he had practically manufactured Joice Heth. "Newspaper and social controversy on the subject (and seldom have vastly more important matters been so largely discussed) served my purpose as 'a showman' by keeping my name before the public," Barnum wrote when he finally spoke out.

About Barnum's cleverness, there can be no doubt. New Yorkers, convinced by Bennett that Barnum had duped them outrageously, were not outraged at Barnum. Instead, they admired his cleverness; they chuckled appreciatively over the colossal hoax he had pulled off. It took a mighty clever man to do that, they reasoned. And so began the birth of a new legend—that of P. T. Barnum, the wizard of show business.

Chapter **5**

Circus and Museum

After the death of Joice Heth, Barnum fell on hard times. He had picked up an Italian juggler, whom he had renamed Signor Vivalla, and he toured the eastern seaboard, exhibiting the Signor's talents. A mere juggler, however, was a pallid attraction compared to a wrinkled crone who hadn't been 161 years old and hadn't been George Washington's nurse. Business was not good; and in April, 1836, Barnum ventured for the first time into the world of the circus. He met and became the partner of Aaron Turner, one of the first circus proprietors in America. Turner would go to any extreme to obtain publicity. A favorite saying of his was: "All we need to insure success is notoriety." Barnum, who had acted on the same principle by instinct, received some advanced schooling in the art of notoriety from Turner.

Having learned about the world of the circus from Turner, Barnum cut loose and organized his own circus, traveling through the Southern states. In Camden, S. C., when his Negro singer decamped just before the show, Barnum blacked his own face, went on stage, and sang the advertised songs—"Zip Coon," "The Raccoon Hunt, or Sitting on a Rail," and "Gittin' Up Stairs." He did so well that his songs were encored vigorously.

His circus, however, did not do so well. In the spring of 1837, after taking his show down the Mississippi to New Orleans, Barnum disbanded it in disgust and returned to New York. He had $2,500 in savings and advertised for a business in which to invest his money. Naturally, there was no lack of takers; everyone in New York, it seemed, was eager to make use of Barnum's $2,500. Barnum weighed the offers and finally made a selection. He decided to risk his money in the enterprise of a German manufacturer who was making waterproof blacking for boots, Cologne water, and bear's grease. After a few months, the German skipped out of the country, leaving Barnum out of pocket $2,500 and holding nothing more substantial than a pot of bear's grease.

Turning back to show business, Barnum rented Vauxhall Garden and put on variety acts. Some of his performers, exhibited on a New York stage for the first time, later were to become famous; but this, at the moment, did Barnum no good. The public wouldn't come to see them, receipts were poor, and he had to close the show. He took some of his cast on tour, but four months later, in New Orleans, he found himself with the same $100 in his pocket with which he had started. He made only expenses. This was not progress. He returned to New York and obtained the agency to sell *Sear's Pictorial Illustrations of The Bible*. He advertised widely, appointed agents and subagents in other cities, and sold thousands of books. Unfortunately several of his agents cheated him; he lost all his profits and all his capital; and once more he faced financial ruin.

At the age of 31 Barnum seemed to have run out of prospects. He had made a lot of money in some of his ventures, but he had not managed to keep it. Whenever he had trusted partners and business associates, he had been swindled. He was a married man with two daughters to support and a third soon to be born. He had to grasp at almost any kind of work to make a living. For $4 a week, he wrote advertisements for the Bowery Amphitheater; he also wrote occasional articles for the Sunday newspapers. These were poor-paying jobs, but important. Not only did they keep Barnum's family in food, but through them he came to know newspaper editors and to make friends in the newspaper world. These new friends soon were to be invaluable. It was, in fact, as a result of them that he picked up an important item of information: the American Museum was up for sale.

The Museum had been founded in 1810, the year of Barnum's birth, and it had become New York's greatest storehouse of curiosities. Its founder, a man named Scudder, had spent some $50,000 gathering strange specimens to exhibit from all quarters of the world. When he died, he had left a fortune and the Museum to his children. His heirs naturally appreciated the fortune, but they had no great interest in the Museum and no knowledge of how to run it. As a result, the Museum had been losing money steadily, and the Scudder estate was anxious to dispose of it for $15,000. This struck Barnum as a real bargain; and he began visiting the Museum regularly, trying to decide for himself why it wasn't making money. The cause, he found, was simple: the management had no vigor, no imagination.

These were qualities Barnum knew he could supply. All he needed was to get possession of the Museum. This appeared impossible. Barnum was church-mouse poor; and when he confided his intentions to a friend, the friend reacted with natural incredulity.

"You *buy* the American Museum?" he asked Barnum. "What do you intend to buy it with?"

"*Brass*," replied Barnum, with emphasis, "for gold and silver I have none."

Barnum studied hard on the problem of how he was to buy the $15,000 Museum collection with no cash. Control of the collections was in the hands of the Scudder estate administrator, John Heath. But, Barnum learned, the Museum did not own its exhibition hall at Broadway and Ann Street; it merely rented space in the building there, which was owned by Francis W. Olmsted, a retired merchant. Barnum decided to approach Olmsted first.

He did not know the merchant, and he didn't know anyone who did. He decided, therefore, to outline his proposition in a letter. His task was to try to convince Olmsted that he, Barnum, was a bargain, even without money. He told Olmsted that he wanted to buy the Museum collection; but since he lacked the funds, he was proposing that Olmsted buy it for him. He cited his record as a showman and expressed his conviction that the only thing needed to make the Museum highly profitable was energy and devotion to business. These Barnum proposed to sup-

[65]

ply. For his services, Olmsted was to permit him to take $12.50 a week from the profits to support his family; all of the remaining profits were to go to Olmsted until the cost of buying the collection and the rent on the building had been paid. When these charges had been met, the Museum was to become Barnum's property. If at any time he failed to make his payments, he was to lose all that he had put in, to withdraw from the management, and to leave the Museum to Olmsted. Barnum emphasized strongly the only selling point he had: if his plan succeeded, Olmsted would have a permanent tenant for his building. This would be a pure gain for Olmsted; for, as thing were going, it was almost certain the Museum would fail and Olmsted would have an empty building on his hands.

Barnum delivered this highly novel proposal in person at Olmsted's door. Soon he received an appointment for an interview. Olmsted questioned him closely. Barnum answered all his questions frankly; and when Olmsted asked him for references, he named a long list of showmen and newspapermen. Olmsted set a day for them to call on him; Barnum was to return himself the following day and learn the verdict.

With impatience and anxiety, Barnum waited for the appointed time. When it came, he presented himself to Olmsted. The merchant frowned at him and snapped:

"I don't like your references, Mr. Barnum."

Barnum, surprised and shocked, stammered:

"I regret to hear that."

At the look on Barnum's face, Olmsted broke out laughing.

"They all speak too well of you," he said. "In fact, they talk as if they were all partners of yours, and intended to share in the profits."

Barnum was both relieved and delighted. He knew that, if Olmsted was playing this kind of a game with him, Olmsted was going to accept his proposition. The details were quickly arranged. Everything, indeed, appeared to be settled when Olmsted brought up one final point. Did Barnum have some piece of unencumbered real estate that he could offer as security? Barnum had nothing. All his real estate holdings in Connecticut were mortgaged to the hilt. With a sinking sensation of despair, he saw his golden opportunity slipping away. Then he had an inspiration. He still owned Ivy Island, the five acres of snakes and poison ivy that had represented his grandfather Taylor's practical joke on him when he entered the world. Ivy Island wasn't mortgaged because no one in Connecticut, knowing the property, would lend a dime on it. But Olmsted didn't know that. Gravely, Barnum offered him Ivy Island as security; and just as seriously, considering himself protected, Olmsted accepted it.

Having obtained Olmsted's agreement, Barnum next approached Heath. After some dickering, the Scudder estate administrator agreed to sell Barnum the Museum's collection for $12,000. Barnum was to take possession on Nov. 15, 1841, and a day was appointed to draw up the agreement with Olmsted. When the hour came, however, Heath appeared with a shocker. He had had a better offer, he said, and he had sold the collection to the New York Museum Company for $15,000. He had accepted a $1,000

[67]

deposit. Barnum appealed to Heath's honor to stand by their agreement, but Heath pointed out he hadn't committed himself in writing and he felt bound to do the best he could for Scudder's orphan daughters. The new agreement satisfied Olmsted, for he would now have a permanent tenant for his building without any risk on his part. Only Barnum was the loser, and his throat had really been cut.

Anyone who thought that Barnum would take such a double crossing lying down simply didn't know Barnum. He scurried around to find out all he could about the directors of the New York Museum Company. The chairman of the board of directors, he learned, had headed a bank that had failed; the other directors were all stock speculators, men out for a fast killing in the market. Their plan was to combine the American Museum with Peale's Museum, which the chairman already controlled, then to issue $50,000 worth of stock to the public. The directors expected to squirrel away about $30,000 for themselves, and they frankly didn't care what happened to the stock, the public, or the Museum after that. Learning these details, Barnum went to see all his newspaper friends and planned a newspaper campaign exposing the deal.

Before the press attack began, he made one other move. He went to see Heath and asked him when the speculators were to pay the additional $14,000 and actually take over the Museum. Heath said payment was to be made December 26th. Barnum prophesied the money would never be paid. As for himself, he said, he was planning to leave December 27th with his circus for a tour of the Southern states. If he couldn't purchase the Museum by that date, he would never buy it. Heath was shaken by Barnum's confident declaration that the speculators would default on their agreement and begged him to stay until December 27th. Heath agreed to give Barnum an option, this time in writing. Before leaving Heath, Barnum warned him that everything must be kept secret. Heath agreed; and Barnum, when his friends asked him, shook his head sorrowfully and confessed that he had lost all chance to buy the Museum.

Then the press barrage broke against the New York Museum Company. Barnum penned scathing attacks on the speculators as a bunch of broken-down bank directors out to fleece the public. The campaign soon hurt. Public confidence was shaken. On December 1st Barnum was invited to call upon the directors of the company to learn something that would be to his advantage. He accepted the invitation and found the directors, well knowing who had aroused the press against them, prepared to buy him off. They offered him the post as manager of their combined museums at his own asking price of $3,000 a year. Barnum accepted, but he stipulated that he wasn't to begin his duties until January 1, 1842.

As Barnum was leaving, the chairman of the board remarked pleasantly:

"Of course, Mr. Barnum, we shall have no more of your squibs through the newspapers."

"I ever try to serve the interests of my employers," Barnum replied, a remark that didn't mean all it seemed to mean.

The directors thought they had outfoxed Barnum and

[69]

could deal with him later at their leisure. "They thought they had caught me securely," Barnum wrote. "I *knew* that I had caught *them*."

Unaware of Barnum's secret option with Heath and thinking Barnum was their own hired hand, the speculators decided to wait until after the first of the year before offering their stock to the public. By that time prospective buyers would forget Barnum's charges, they reasoned, and Heath wouldn't mind a slight delay in getting the balance of the money. So the December 26th deadline passed, and on the morning of December 27th, Barnum and his lawyer met with Heath and Olmsted in Olmsted's suite on Park Place. The payment to Heath was made, and at two o'clock in the afternoon, Barnum became the owner of the American Museum. His first act was to sit down and write a kindly little note to the stock speculators whom he had just outwitted. His note read:

"American Museum, New York, Dec. 27, 1841. To the President and Directors of the New York Museum:

"Gentlemen:—It gives me great pleasure to inform you that you are placed upon the Free List of this establishment until further notice.

P. T. Barnum, Proprietor"

Chapter **6**

The Talk of New York

W hen Barnum took control of the American Museum on January 1, 1842, he had just one goal in mind—to make it and him the talk of New York. Before Barnum bought the Museum the exterior of the building was plain and unadorned, displaying just two words: American Museum. There was nothing to attract attention, nothing to excite the public. Barnum quickly changed that. He displayed large posters advertising his attractions. He obtained the worst band he could find and placed it on the balcony outside the building with instructions to play as loudly as it could. The noise, he figured, would certainly attract attention and let the public know his Museum was there. At night, with the aid of huge Drummond lights, the first New York had seen, he illuminated the outside of the building and the entire Broadway area for several blocks around. By such devices, he swiftly made the public aware that Barnum's American Museum, as it now came to be known, promised variety, interest, and excitement.

The Museum was located in the heart of New York. Directly opposite it at Broadway and Ann was the city's most famous hotel, the Astor House. Across the street was St. Paul's Church. Four blocks north was the best restaurant, Delmonico's; and in the same district, handy to Barnum's influence, were the offices of the *Tribune,* the *Herald,* and other newspapers. The location of the Museum, was ideal. The Museum had one other distinct advantage: it filled a vacuum. New York in that day had no zoo to exhibit specimens of wild life; it had no Metropolitan Museum of Art in which to display great paintings; no American Museum of Natural History to illustrate for man the stages of his past. Barnum's American Museum filled the gap.

Under Scudder's management, the Museum had exhibited relics sent in from all sections of America and curiosities obtained from sea captains who had made voyages to the Far East and other lands. Its main attractions included a variety of stuffed animals, a few live ones such as an anaconda and a tame alligator, and its gallery of portraits of national heroes. All of this was fine; but Barnum, who as a boy had sought out the "two-tailed dog," instinctively wanted something novel to excite the public imagination and draw customers.

He soon found what he was seeking. An artist had constructed a fine-scale model of Niagara Falls with the cataract, the trees, and rocks and buildings in the vicinity all reproduced in exact proportion. The Falls were, of course, one of the wonders of America, a natural phenomenon of which Americans were most proud. Realizing this, Barnum saw possibilities in the model and bought it for $200. Then

[72]

he devised a way to get real water to flow over the falls. All he needed to produce this novelty was a single barrel of water and a pump. Water was pumped from the barrel over the falls; it fell into a secret reservoir, was circulated back to the barrel and pumped over the falls again. The barrel and pump, of course, were kept well out of public view, while Barnum proclaimed in gaudy advertisements: "The Great Model of Niagara Falls, With Real Water!" The public generally was deceived into believing that Barnum somehow had managed to crowd into the America Museum a colossal replica of the great falls. Only after visitors had paid their 25 cents for admission did they discover that the water spilled over the falls for a distance of only 18 inches!

"I confess I felt somewhat ashamed," Barnum wrote later of this deception that he had practiced upon the public; but he consoled himself with the thought that if visitors found his model of Niagara Falls "rather 'small potatoes,' they had the whole Museum to fall back upon. . ." And the educational displays in the Museum, Barnum argued in self-justification, were certainly worth a quarter of anyone's money.

Barnum, the perfect showman, was the first great American advertising genius; he always found ways of using words to make whatever he had to exhibit seem greater, grander, and decidedly more novel than it actually was. For example, he advertised that the Museum boasted among its novelties "an aerial garden." The public naturally had some difficulty imagining what a garden in the air would be like and came to satisfy its curiosity. What it found, on the roof of the museum, was nothing more extraordinary than two tubs, each containing a stunted and faded cedar, and ten or twelve pots of wilted flowers. A few chairs and tables were scattered around this "aerial garden," and there those who liked ice cream could sit and eat it while they marveled at the wonderful uses of advertising.

So resourceful was Barnum, so numerous his devices, that soon all New York was wondering, "What will Barnum do next?" But not even the wiliest mind in New York could have foreseen the unique use Barnum was to make of a bricklayer.

One morning a strong, robust-looking man appeared at the Museum office and asked Barnum for money.

"Why don't you work and earn a living?" Barnum inquired.

"I can't find anything to do," the man said. "I would be glad to work for a dollar a day if I could find something to do."

Barnum handed the man a quarter, told him to go and get some breakfast, and then come back.

"I will give you a good light job," Barnum promised, "and I'll give you a dollar-and-a-half a day, too."

This was a good wage in those days, and the muscular man, having eaten his breakfast, returned to see what kind of a job Barnum had to offer. Barnum was waiting for him with five bricks. Barnum told his new employee to pick up the bricks, then led him outside. He stopped at the curb at the corner of Broadway and Ann, directly in front of the Museum, and instructed the man to place a brick on the curb. Then three other bricks were placed, one at the corner of Broadway and Vesey, another in front of the

Astor House, the last in front of St. Paul's Church.

"Now," said Barnum to the bewildered man, "take your fifth brick and march rapidly to the first one you laid down; exchange them. Go on to the next and do the same,

Perplexed passersby watched the man exchange brick for brick.

and so on with all four, and keep on repeating the round but say nothing to anyone."

"What is it all for?" the man asked.

"Never mind," Barnum told him. "It is a bit of my fun, but to be worth anything to me, you must look solemn, seem to be as deaf as a post, pay no attention to anyone, and answer no questions."

Barnum's husky new hired hand shrugged his shoulders, agreed to do just what Barnum said, and started his novel bricklaying. In practically no time at all, his strange actions began to attract a small crowd of spectators. What was the man doing putting down bricks, picking them up, putting them down again? What was the sense of it? What could he be up to? Intrigued, the crowd grew. Within a half hour, some 500 persons were clustered on the sidewalks watching the mute and mysterious shuffler of bricks. Faithful to Barnum's orders, the man ignored them. At the end of an hour, he went to the doors of the Museum, presented a ticket and was admitted. The crowd, thinking the solution to the mystery must lie inside the Museum, bought tickets and followed the man. After staying in the Museum for 15 minutes, just long enough to give all who were going to buy tickets a chance to buy them, the bricklayer returned to the street, repeated his mystifying performance, and lured a new crowd.

This old stunt continued for several days and never failed to draw crowds of several hundred persons, a large percentage of whom were lured through the doors of Barnum's American Museum at 25 cents a head. The success of the scheme was finally the cause of its undoing. It drew so many spectators that, on one occasion, all the streets around the Museum became clogged with the watching crowd, traffic could not proceed, and the police protested. Naturally, the newspapers took notice of the stunt that had drawn such huge crowds; it became the talk of the town, and the names P. T. Barnum and the American Museum were, it seemed, on almost everyone's lips.

Barnum's success was reflected in a volume of museum-goers such as had never been known before. Any other man might have been content, but Barnum always wanted to make a big success bigger and he exercised all his ingenuity to increase the flow of cash. He had decided originally to invest all the excess profits of his first year in advertising, but now the profits were so large Barnum was taxed to find enough ways to advertise. This happy problem led him to take another fantastic step. He decided to improve on the ordinary display posters. Hiring an artist, he had the man paint huge, vivid panels of all the strange animals in creation. In a single night he had workmen cover the entire outside surface of the Museum with these paintings. Since he had this done without advance notice or fanfare, New Yorkers the next morning were startled by the sight of the staid Museum of the night before broken out into a positive rash of jungle animals. People came to stare at the paintings, to marvel at the strange beasts—and to buy tickets so that they might see all these wonders inside the Museum for themselves. Barnum estimated that the paintings increased his profits by $100 a day; and although the novelty eventually wore off, receipts remained pegged at the new level, for Barnum's marvelous animals caught the eye of every immigrant and every stranger arriving in the city of New York.

Barnum opened his Museum at sunrise and kept it open until late at night. He worked practically around the clock, determined to pay off his debt to Olmsted and obtain clear

[77]

possession of the Museum for himself. While he worked, his mind was always feverishly devising new schemes, new attractions, new ways to catch the public eye and hold the public interest. It was the world's way, Barnum later wrote, "to promise everything for next to nothing," and he was a positive genius at this art.

Typical is the story of the Negro violinist. Barnum had hired the violinist, who had had foreign musical training and possessed a great reputation in musical circles, to perform in the Lecture Room of the Museum. He advertised his new attraction widely, but the public did not seem to be passionately interested in hearing a violinist. Receipts did not increase. Barnum studied the problem, and he finally, as he always did, hit upon a scheme. He issued orders that the large colored posters outside the Museum showing the violinist in action were to be turned upside down. This created the impression that the violinist played standing on his head, and in no time the Museum was crowded with throngs eager to see this novel sight. Of course, Barnum had not *said* that the musician played standing upon his head; he had merely encouraged the public to leap to this fascinating, false conclusion. And, of course, once the public had paid the price of admission, it could console itself with all those other fine attractions Barnum's Museum offered.

Barnum overlooked no opportunity to pack the American Museum with as many visitors as could possibly be crammed inside its walls. On his first Fourth of July as manager, he vividly demonstrated his skill in attracting the public and in handling it to his own best advantage

[78]

once it was attracted. Realizing the publicity value of the United States flag, Barnum had made plans in advance to attract crowds to his Museum by erecting a string of huge flags across Broadway. He intended to fasten one end of the string to the top of the Museum building and the other end to a tree in St. Paul's Churchyard. Several days in advance he visited the vestrymen of the church and asked for permission to use their tree. The churchmen were shocked, outraged. It would be positively irreligious, they said, to use a church tree for such a commercial purpose. Barnum absolutely could *not* tie his flags to their tree.

Acting like a man who didn't understand the word "no," Barnum calmly went ahead with his plans. On the morning of the Fourth, he ordered the string of flags hoisted across Broadway, with one end tied to the churchyard tree, just as he had originally planned. The flag display attracted a large crowd, and ticket business at the Museum began to step up to a merry tempo. It didn't take the church fathers long to become aware of what was happening; at 9:30 in the morning two apoplectic vestrymen stormed into Barnum's office. This was an outrage, they shouted. Barnum must give orders at once to detach the string of flags from church property. Barnum was most polite. He offered to go out to the street with the vestrymen and see what could be done.

Once outside, Barnum stood and looked at the string of flags admiringly, just as if he had never seen such a gorgeous sight before. He remarked that the flags really made a beautiful sight. The vestrymen were not to be put off. They demanded that the flags come down. A reasonable man, Barnum suggested to the irate vestrymen that perhaps they should think twice and cooperate a little. He pointed out that he had always had his loud band stop its "Free Music for the Millions" during their services. It was little enough he asked in return, the mere loan of a limb of their tree. At this, seeing that Barnum did not intend to take the flags down, One of the vestrymen lost all patience and shouted that if Barnum did not take the flags down, he would *cut them down.*

This was the opening for which Barnum had been waiting. A large crowd had gathered to listen to the dispute, and Barnum set about enlisting it in his service. Dramatically whipping off his coat, he rolled up his shirt sleeves and shouted:

"I should like to see you dare to cut down the flag on the Fourth of July. You must be a Britisher to make such a threat, but I'll show you a thousand pairs of Yankee hands in two minutes, if you dare to take down the stars and stripes on this great birthday of American freedom!"

In an instant, the crowd was with Barnum. Menacing scowls, angry mutters, and threats greeted the vestrymen on every side. Frightened, the two men of the church slunk away, and Barnum was left to enjoy his triumph—and a record crowd for his Museum.

So huge was the crowd, in fact, that the Museum couldn't hold it all, and the sale of tickets had to be stopped. This left several thousand potential customers waiting on the street outside—a sight that, as Barnum wrote, was "exceedingly harrowing to my feelings."

In desperation, Barnum tried to think up a way to get

the throng inside the Museum to leave more quickly. He summoned his carpenter and ordered a temporary flight of stairs built at the rear of the building. This was a major project, and it was not until after three o'clock in the afternoon that this emergency rear exit was completed. Much business had been lost.

Barnum, however, considered the rear stairway a good investment for the future, and indeed it was not long before he had occasion for its use. On the following St. Patrick's Day, a large portion of the city's heavy Irish population decided to visit the Museum. Barnum had been informed in advance, and he had the rear exit opened. Despite this, by noon, the Museum was so crowded that once more the sale of tickets had to be stopped.

Sensing that the throng inside was in no mood to leave, Barnum rushed to the rear exit and asked his employees how many persons had gone out that way. Just three, he was told. He looked around him and found that many of the visitors had come equipped with box lunches and dinners, apparently prepared to make a day of it and to stay into the night. This would never do. It meant that Barnum could never get enough of the crowd outside the building so that he could begin selling tickets again.

A stratagem was needed, and Barnum's brain worked furiously, as it always did in time of emergencies, to come up with the necessary trick. Hastily summoning his sign painter, he ordered him to print in large, bold letters this notice: "To the Egress." This sign, he had nailed above the rear exit.

To his Irish customers, the word "Egress" was a strange

one indeed. They had no suspicion that it meant exit, and they stopped and spelled it out and wondered about its meaning. "Sure," many of them said, "That's an animal we haven't seen." And so they hurried to the door and passed

"Sure," customers said, "here's an animal we haven't seen."

through expecting to see a new wonder; they found themselves, before they quite knew what had happened, outside the Museum on Ann Street, with no chance of getting back. That day, Barnum really did a roaring business.

Such brilliant strokes of showmanship made Barnum

the talk of the city, but they were little more than a pre-
lude to a Barnum-promoted controversy that was to set all
New York by the ears. This was his exhibition of the so-
called Fejee Mermaid.

In the early summer of 1842, only a few months after
Barnum had taken over the Museum, a man named Moses
Kimball brought Barnum a figure that was supposed to be a
preserved mermaid. Kimball, the proprietor of the Boston
Museum, recited a long history, detailing how the object
came into his possession. It seemed that the captain of a
Boston ship, putting in at Calcutta in 1817, had been offered the mermaid, which, he was assured, was a genuine
specimen that had been obtained from Japanese sailors.
The price asked was $6,000, and the ship's captain, cer-
tain that a fortune was to be made from exhibiting such a
creature, the like of which man had never seen before,
looted the ship's funds and made the purchase. The owners
of the vessel were decidedly disenchanted with their skip-
per, who failed to make a fortune exhibiting the mermaid;
he spent the rest of his life working off his $6,000 debt. The
sea captain never abandoned the idea, however, that the
mermaid was an exceedingly valuable piece of property.
He preserved it carefully; and when he died, he left this
most precious of his possessions to his son. The son, taking
a dim view of his father's treasure, sold the mermaid to
Kimball. And Kimball brought it to Barnum.

Just looking at the thing, Barnum easily could see
that man had never witnessed such an oddity before. For
the Fejee Mermaid was a creature with a monkey's head
on a fish's body. The spine extended in one seemingly un-

broken line to the base of the skull. The shoulders were covered with animal hair, yet, when viewed through a microscope, fish scales became apparent beneath the hair. The whole specimen, some three feet long, was dried up and black, with a hideously ugly face. The mouth was wide open, revealing bestial teeth, and the whole expression seemed to be that of an animal that had died in extreme agony. The creature had thin, misshapen arms, with fingers of hideous length at the end of twisted, distorted hands. The entire torso merged into a tapering, scaly, fish-like tail, equipped with weird fins.

Examining Kimball's monstrosity, Barnum could find no indications that it had been man-made; he could see nothing to indicate that its two unlikely parts had been pieced or sewn together. Not trusting entirely to his own opinion, however, he decided to seek that of a naturalist who often advised him on such matters. This expert examined the mermaid and announced that he couldn't find anything to indicate it had been manufactured, but he was convinced it must have been. He had never heard, he said, of a monkey with such peculiar teeth, arms and hands, or of a fish with such peculiar fins. Barnum wasn't satisfied. Why, he wanted to know, did the expert think the mermaid had been manufactured when he could discover no evidence of it?

"Because I don't believe in mermaids," said the naturalist.

"That is no reason at all," said Barnum, "and therefore I'll believe in the mermaid, and hire it."

Barnum's will to believe obviously fitted nicely with

his desire to find ever new and stranger attractions for his Museum. He could smell the makings of a fortune in the Fejee Mermaid, but the business would have to be very carefully and delicately handled. The public, naturally skeptical where mermaids were concerned, would have to be convinced, not that mermaids actually existed, but that there was just the *possibility* that they *might*. Once Barnum could get that idea across, there would be a grand controversy, and everybody would want to come and see the mermaid and make up his mind for himself.

"Some extraordinary means must be resorted to," was the way Barnum put it, "and I saw no better method than to 'start the ball a-rolling' at some distance from the centre of attraction."

Now began an innocent-appearing, slowly creeping campaign to acquaint New Yorkers with the possibility of mermaids. First there appeared a newsletter, ostensibly written to the New York *Herald* by a correspondent in Montgomery, Alabama. The letter described the state of trade in Montgomery, the condition of the crops, the political situation, and near the end it mentioned a strange circumstance. A "Dr. Griffin," of the Lyceum of Natural History in London, had recently returned from Pernambuco with a most remarkable curiosity, a real mermaid found by the Chinese in the Fiji Islands and preserved by them. "Dr. Griffin" was taking his unique find with him to London for exhibition.

A week later, another New York newspaper ran a similar newsletter supposedly sent it by an informant in Charlestown, S. C. This letter, too, just happened to mention that "Dr. Griffin" and his mermaid were passing through Charleston. Another week went by, and another letter appeared in a third New York newspaper. This one, datelined Washington, also told about the discovery of the mermaid and announced the further interesting fact that "Dr. Griffin" was going to visit New York on his way back to London. It was hoped, said the writer, that the public of New York might have a chance to view this most unusual specimen before "Dr. Griffin" took his mermaid to London forever.

Barnum, of course, had written all three letters. In those days, newspapers did not have their own news-gathering services, and so they were in the habit of printing letters sent to them by readers in distant cities, giving news of local affairs. Barnum had taken advantage of this custom by drafting the bogus newsletters himself, mailing them to friends, and having the friends re-mail them to the New York papers. By this device, he had obtained a triple announcement of the "discovery" of the Fejee Mermaid. And so, having paved the way, he was ready to throw his publicity campaign into high gear.

Only a few days after the last blurb had appeared in the New York press, Barnum's old friend and collaborator, Levi Lyman, appeared in Philadelphia. Lyman, the smooth talker who had convinced the world that Joice Heth was George Washington's nurse, registered at one of the most prominent Philadelphia hostelries as "Dr. Griffin," of Pernambuco, bound for London. In his short stay, "Dr. Griffin," impressed Philadelphians. He was a gentleman with the most silken manners, the most engaging personality; everybody liked him, and everybody was sorry when it came time, at last for him to leave. "Dr. Griffin" seemed sorry, too. As he paid his hotel bill, he thanked the landlord for the excellent service he had received and, just to show his goodwill, invited his host up to his room "to see something that will surprise you."

The landlord went, saw, and was truly surprised. So great, indeed, was the impression made upon him by the Fejee Mermaid that he begged "Dr. Griffin" to let him bring in a few of his friends to see this once-in-a-lifetime sight. The genial "Dr. Griffin" agreed. Now it just so happened that some of the landlord's good friends were editors; so it came about that the Philadelphia press broke out into a rash of stories about the Fejee Mermaid.

The newspapers in New York naturally took notice of the excitement and the controversy that raged for days in the Philadelphia press. In the midst of the agitation, with perfect timing, "Dr. Griffin" arrived upon the scene and registered at the Pacific Hotel on Greenwich Street. Word soon got around that he was there, reporters flocked to his door, and in a matter of hours the front pages of the New York newspapers were splattered with the fascinating story of the discovery of the Fejee Mermaid.

During all of this buildup, Barnum had kept himself carefully in the background, and no one in New York had any suspicion that the promoter of Joice Heth was also the promoter of the Fejee Mermaid. But the time was now at hand for Barnum to emerge from the shadows. He had had a pamphlet written and printed to demonstrate that it was *possible* there were such creatures as mermaids. Artists had drawn three pictures, *showing* mermaids flitting about in the ocean, and Barnum had had the pictures engraved for reproduction in his pamphlet. He had had 10,000 copies of the pamphlet printed. All was set for the last big publicity push. At this point, Barnum made a round of personal calls on the editors of the three New York Sunday newspapers.

He had hoped, he told each of them sadly, that he would be able to exhibit the Fejee Mermaid at his Museum. But "Dr. Griffin" had decided that, as the agent of the London Lyceum, it would not be ethical for him to permit such a display in America. Since, therefore, Barnum would not be able to exhibit the mermaid, he was making his friend (the editor to whom he happened at the moment to be talking) a present of an engraving he had had made and which was now no longer of any use to him. Each of the editors accepted Barnum's thoughtful gift. On the morning of Sunday, July 17, 1842, each of the three New York newspapers proudly displayed a picture and story about the Fejee Mermaid.

"Each editor supposed he was giving his readers an exclusive treat in the mermaid line," Barnum wrote, "but when they came to discover that I had played the same game with three different papers, they pronounced it a *scaly* trick."

With the publication of the three articles, Barnum wrote, "the mermaid fever was getting pretty well up." To raise it a few degrees higher, Barnum hired boys to distribute his 10,000 mermaid pamphlets in all the principal hotels, stores, and restaurants.

New York was now decidedly mermaid-conscious, and

Barnum decided it was time to reap the rewards of his labor. Still keeping as much in the background as possible, he rented the Concert Hall on Broadway and inserted in the newspapers advertisements to the effect that the noted "Dr. Griffin," yielding reluctantly to popular demand, would exhibit the Fejee Mermaid there "positively for one week only!" The eminent naturalist also, the advertisement informed New Yorkers, would place on exhibition some of his other remarkable discoveries: a creature described as the connecting link between the seal and the duck, a species of flying fish that undoubtedly was the link between fish and bird, the paddle tail snake from South America, and other equally marvellous creatures.

What New Yorker, in that day, could resist the temptation to see such sights? Few could, and few did. Concert Hall was crowded as soon as "Dr. Griffin" and the Fejee Mermaid moved in. Barnum observed the performance from afar with considerable anxiety, for he wrote: "I could not help fearing that some of the Joice Heth victims would discover in Professor Griffin the exhibitor of the 'nurse of Washington,' but happily no such catastrophe occurred." Levi Lyman was his usual suave, courteous, distinguished self; he *looked* the part of "Dr. Griffin," of the London Lyceum of Natural History," and no New Yorker apparently suspected that he wasn't.

The extremely profitable one-week stand of "Dr. Griffin" and the Fejee Mermaid in Concert Hall was followed by a new announcement, one that shed light on everything. Barnum informed the public that he had at last, but only after great difficulty and expense, succeeded in persuading the renowned "Dr. Griffin" to exhibit the Fejee Mermaid at Barnum's American Museum, where this freak of nature in the future could be seen *daily*—and *at no extra charge*. Barnum had gone to infinite pains to bait his hook; the press and public of New York had swallowed it; and now he was ready to pull in the suckers.

Crowds flocked to his American Museum in unprecedented numbers. Throughout New York, throughout the nation, debate raged: mermaids—were they or weren't they? Papers all over the country picked up items from the New York press about the great mermaid controversy, and Barnum and his American Museum became household words.

Barnum's success with the Fejee Mermaid was a happy time, marred only by isolated instances of skepticism. One day, a critical viewer of the mermaid said to Barnum:

"I lived two years on the Fiji Islands, and I never heard of any such thing as a mermaid."

"There's no accounting for some men's ignorance," Barnum told him.

On another occasion, a group of medical students entered the exhibition hall just at a time when the bogus "Dr. Griffin" had left his charge for a minute. Taking advantage of his absence, the students slipped off the glass case protecting the Mermaid, placed a partly smoked cigar in her mouth and replaced the case. The sight of the Mermaid smoking a cigar quickly attracted an even larger crowd than usual. When Levi Lyman returned to the hall in his role of "Dr. Griffin," he assumed that all of these good people were waiting for him to tell them about the Mermaid, and so he promptly launched into his spiel. He had just described how the Mermaid had been taken in a fishermen's net in the Fiji Islands and "lived for upwards of three hours after its capture," when one of the spectators interrupted him.

"Was her ladyship smoking the same cigar when she was captured that she is enjoying at present?" he asked.

This was the first time that Lyman had noticed the cigar, the first he was aware of the trick that had been played on him. He broke out into a cold dripping sweat, and it was, as Barnum wrote, "probably the first and only time in his life that he was completely nonplussed, and could not utter a word in reply."

Barnum could afford to laugh at such minor misadventures, for the Fejee Mermaid was a veritable gold mine. Though Barnum himself never had any real illusions about the Mermaid, considering her the work of some clever Japanese artist, New Yorkers, their curiosity aroused by Barnum's clever publicity, continued to flock to see her. Barnum gratefully recorded the result in his ledgers. In the four weeks preceding the Mermaid's arrival at the Museum, receipts had totaled only $1,272; in the four weeks after the appearance of the fish-lady, they leaped to $3,-341.93. Barnum was in a fair way to pay off his $15,000 debt to Olmsted, and he bent all his energies to this task.

The merchant who had financed him in acquiring the Museum paid him occasional visits to see how things were going. One day he surprised Barnum munching on a cold corned-beef sandwich he had brought from home.

"Is this the way the proprietor of the American Museum eats his lunch?" Olmsted asked.

"I haven't eaten a warm dinner, except on Sundays, since I bought the Museum," Barnum replied; "and what is more, I don't intend to until I have paid for it."

This may have been a slight Barnum exaggeration of the truth; but the answer pleased Olmsted, who clapped Barnum on the shoulder and exclaimed in delight:

"Ah, you are safe and will pay for it inside the year."

In this, he was a true prophet. Barnum's receipts for 1842, his first year, were $27,912.62. He had been so successful that he easily paid off his debt to Olmsted and became the sole owner of the Museum.

He was ready for his littlest—and one of his greatest—triumphs.

Chapter 7

General Tom Thumb

In November, 1842, with the Fejee Mermaid packing them in at the American Museum, Barnum went to Albany on business. His ever-active mind was already seeking out his next attraction, and he had a fairly good idea what it might be. From his relations in Connecticut, he had heard a story that fascinated him and that suggested a possible new means of profit for P. T. Barnum and his American Museum.

A Bridgeport couple, Mr. and Mrs. Sherwood E. Stratton, had a son, a bright and charming and healthy child who, for some mysterious reason, had stopped growing a few months after birth. He was a midget. To the residents of Bridgeport, the tiny boy was a great curiosity, and the thought naturally occurred to Barnum: Would it be possible, with some expert showmanship, to turn him into as great a curiosity for New Yorkers?

There was only one way of finding out, and Barnum determined to go and see for himself. On his way back home from Albany, therefore, he made a visit to Bridgeport and put up at the Franklin Hotel, then being run by his brother, Philo F. Barnum. Philo hunted up the midget, brought him to the hotel, and introduced him to Barnum.

"He was the smallest child I ever saw that could walk alone," Barnum later reported.

The boy who stood before Barnum was less than two feet tall and weighed only a little more than 15 pounds. He had exceptionally light, flaxen hair and dark, glowing eyes. His cheeks were pink; his complexion, healthy; his body, perfectly formed. There was only one flaw. He was so *tiny*. Looking at him, Barnum was fascinated. He tried to strike up a conversation, but he found that the young midget was quite bashful. Barnum had to coax and wheedle before he could get the child to say that his name was Charles S. Stratton and that he was just five years old.

This bashfulness, charming in its way, might represent a drawback upon the stage, but Barnum, studying the boy, saw that he was alert and bright and felt that the bashfulness could be overcome. Properly managed—and Barnum would see to that—Charles S. Stratton might be quite an attraction for the American Museum. Barnum decided to try the experiment.

The following day, he visited the child's parents and made a deal with them. Barnum would pay all expenses for the boy and his mother, and he would pay in addition $3 a week salary to exhibit the young midget on the stage of his American Museum. It was a bargain if there ever was one; but Barnum, uncertain about the pulling power of a midget with the New York public, bound himself to only a four-week contract.

From the first, Barnum realized that "some license" would have to be taken with the facts. Since the boy was only five years old, the question naturally would arise: How could anyone be certain he *was* a midget? Barnum wrote that he had "the most reliable evidence he had grown little, if any, since he was six months old;" but the New York public especially in view of the Joice Heth and Fejee Mermaid episodes, might not be willing to accept Barnum's "most reliable evidence." Considering the problem, Barnum decided that the best way to settle the question was not to let it be raised. He would proclaim boldy that the boy was 11 years old. That way, the public would be convinced he was really a midget.

With this hurdle cleared, in Barnum's mind at least, the master of the American Museum turned to some other elements of window dressing. Barnum found it difficult to imagine that the American public would become greatly excited about a midget named Charles S. Stratton, of Bridgeport, Connecticut. This name and background was too dull, too ordinary; it lacked the kind of romantic flavor that helps to make a stage personality. Barnum decided to supply the lack, and in handbills that he had distributed all over New York, he announced that he would soon present on the stage of the American Museum "General Tom Thumb," who had "just arrived from England."

This was a double stroke of genius on Barnum's part. The name came straight out of an old nursery rhyme that described a legendary Tom Thumb as being so diminutive he was swallowed by a cow when he crossed the blade of grass she was eating. In happy spoof, Barnum added the grand title of "General," and so the most apt name with which a midget was ever christened was coined—General Tom Thumb. To heighten the appeal, Barnum gave to his newly created "general" a European background. Americans of that period had a great love for foreign importations. Native, domestic products seemed too ordinary, too provincial; but anything coming from Europe seemed to have an air of romance about it. Barnum played up to this public tendency and always tried to give the impression that he had gone to great pains and expense to bring to America the wonders of foreign lands. And so he billed General Tom Thumb as a wonder midget just arrived from England.

Both the name and the English background came as quite a shock to General Tom Thumb and his mother, Mrs. Stratton, when they arrived in New York on Thanksgiving Day, 1842. Tom Thumb's mother didn't very much like the idea of being Mrs. Thumb instead of Mrs. Stratton, but Barnum managed to convince her that this innocent little deception was necessary for the welfare of her boy and that, otherwise, the American public might not be induced to come to see him.

This point won, Barnum set out to train his "diminutive prodigy," as he called the General. He spent long hours "by day and by night" instructing Tom Thumb. Stage roles, new jokes, engaging mannerisms—Barnum taught them all to the tiny actor whom he was about to present upon the stage of the American Museum's Lecture Room. Since General Tom Thumb was exceptionally bright and had a madcap humor all his own, it was not long before he was ready to face the public.

With the date of Tom Thumb's debut approaching, Barnum took "the least of the little men," as he often called the midget, on a tour of newspaper offices. They made a sight, the two of them. Barnum was in every respect a big man—tall, bulky in build, with a massive head crowned by thick, wavy locks of hair. The contrast with Tom Thumb, less than two feet tall, dressed in a gaudy general's uniform, using a foot rule for a cane, was so startling that no one who saw the oddly matched pair could ever possibly forget them.

The impression they made on one New York editor was especially vivid. They arrived at the editor's home just as he and a number of guests were sitting down to dinner. Barnum with one huge hand hoisted Tom Thumb upon the table as if he had been a toy. The roast reached almost to the chest of the midget's vivid uniform. While the dinner guests gaped, Tom Thumb hopped over the roast and skipped among the tumblers, pausing at times to make pert remarks to individual diners. When Barnum finally lifted the saucy little fellow down from the table and went on his way, he left behind him a babble of conversation and the seeds of a newspaper story that was a press agent's dream.

In his advertisements, Barnum proclaimed the uniqueness of Tom Thumb. He challenged the entire world to produce a smaller human being. Taking up the challenge, one tiny actor who had been quite an attraction as a dwarf came to see the General. He departed, shaking his head and vowing that in the future he would have to call himself a giant. Such incidents, promptly reported in the press—

Barnum always saw to that—whipped up the eagerness of New Yorkers to see General Tom Thumb; but to Tom Thumb himself belongs the credit for fanning the blaze of interest that Barnum had aroused. The little man had a wealth of natural talent; and on the stage of Barnum's Lecture Room, he became a small-scale riot.

To emphasize his smallness, Barnum had had built a tiny house, so small a child could have picked it up. In this Tom Thumb moved around as a man might in an ordinary home; he sat in a tiny chair and talked to his audience through a window. With Barnum as his instructor, "the least of the little men" quickly became adept at impersonations. Sometimes he appeared as an English fox hunter in a red coat, drab breeches, and top boots with feet only three inches long. At other times, he dressed up as Napoleon and strutted back and forth across the stage, his little chest puffed out in perfect imitation of the French emperor. He learned to sing and dance, and sometimes he would bounce upon the stage clad in sailor's togs and ready to do a hornpipe; at others, he would break out into the tune of "Yankee Doddle" or, as his repertoire grew, into a wide assortment of "coon songs." Added to all these skills, which Barnum so carefully cultivated, was a saucy wit that was the General's own. He was lightning-fast at repartee, and he got away with sallies for which a normal-sized person almost certainly would have been slapped.

It is little wonder that, with these gifts, "the least of the little men" became from the first one of Barnum's greatest successes. Midgets have always exercised a strange fascination for the public, but Tom Thumb was far from being a mere freak; he was in his own right an engaging character. New Yorkers fell in love with the saucy, witty little fellow, and the well-to-do and the fashionable flocked to see him. Often a long line of fancy carriages lined up before Barnum's Museum, jamming Broadway while the coachmen waited for their employers to tire of marveling over Tom Thumb.

Barnum realized at once, of course, that he had an extremely valuable property on his hands; and when Tom Thumb's first four-week engagement was finished, Barnum hired him to a year-long contract at a raise in pay—to all of $7 a week. In fairness to Barnum, it must be noted that, before the year expired, he changed the contract himself and began paying Tom Thumb $25 a week because "he fairly earned it." He certainly did. Not only did Tom Thumb pack the American Museum for Barnum, but he went on tour, carrying the name of the master showman and the Museum to audiences in other cities throughout the nation.

At the end of the year, Barnum renewed Tom Thumb's contract at a salary of $50 a week and expenses, and began to look around him for new worlds to conquer. The American Museum, less than three years under his management, was running so smoothly and making so much money that Barnum's personal touch was no longer essential. Barnum decided, therefore, to gamble for new and larger stakes. He would take Tom Thumb on a tour of Europe.

With his usual skill, Barnum made the European tour an excuse to whip the public of New York into a final frenzy to see the General. He acted on the golden principle that human nature always wants what it hasn't got or can't get; and so he proclaimed loudly in advertisements that Tom Thumb was leaving, that this was "the last chance" New Yorkers would have to see him. When contrary winds delayed the sailing of the *Yorkshire* packet, on which he had booked passage, Barnum took out more advertisements informing New Yorkers of their great good luck—General Tom Thumb could be seen all day, for just one day more!

The response was all that Barnum could have wished, and he was almost brokenhearted at the necessity of tearing himself away from Tom Thumb's public when the unkind winds at last turned favorable and the sailing no longer could be delayed. Tom Thumb, it was estimated, had drawn some 80,000 persons into Barnum's American Museum; and Barnum kept him on the stage, drawing the very last one of them, until 11 o'clock on the morning of January 19, 1844. With their ship scheduled to sail at noon, even Barnum could delay no longer, and he and his tiny protégé hurried directly from the Museum to the waterfront. Incredible as it may seem today, in this more blasé and sophisticated age, the municipal brass band turned out to escort them, and a crowd of some 10,000 persons massed along the streets and wharves to wave them farewell. Such was the public tribute to Tom Thumb, the tiniest and the mightiest of Barnum's many attractions.

A stormy, 19-day ocean passage brought Barnum, Tom Thumb, and Tom's parents, Mr. and Mrs. Stratton, to Liverpool—and to one of the few periods of black doubt in Barnum's career. Finding himself in a strange land whose customs he did not know, Barnum sank into what, for him, was an unnatural despondency and began to regret that he had ever left home. This mood was caused, in large part at least, by some early indications that the British public might not be as fond of midgets—and of one midget in particular—as New Yorkers had been.

Shortly after Barnum's arrival, a Liverpool showman, who had heard about Tom Thumb, appeared at Barnum's hotel with an offer to hire the little man for a paltry $10 a week. This, to Barnum, was an insult both to pride and pocketbook, and it was difficult to tell which hurt worse. Doubtless the Liverpool showman was seeking to drive a shrewd bargain, but even kindhearted persons didn't seem to think much of Tom Thumb's chances. Barnum and the midget went to the theater and sat in a box that a kind admirer had donated to them. Their neighbors, a wealthy man and woman, were much taken with Tom Thumb. Barnum asked them what they thought about his chance of exhibiting the little General. Innocently, the woman replied that he might be able to charge as much as two-pence a head, but her husband interrupted, chiding her for not knowing anything about business and predicting that the British public would never pay more than a penny to see such a dwarf. Barnum was dismayed. Back at his hotel, as he later confessed, he had "a solitary hearty crying-spell," but he resolved that he would never exhibit Tom Thumb cheaply—never for less than a shilling.

Fired by this determination, Barnum finally shook off his despair and became the old Barnum. He had supplied himself with letters of introduction to influential Britons, and on the advice of some of Liverpool's best families, he

[101]

rented a hall and presented General Tom Thumb in a few exhibitions. Crowds came to see the midget, and Barnum's spirits revived. He was especially cheered when the manager of the Princess's Theatre in London came to steal a look at Tom Thumb and was so impressed he wanted to hire him on the spot. Barnum consented to go to London and permit Tom to make three appearances. These were a decided success and started London tongues wagging in a small way about Barnum's remarkable little man. The manager of the Princess's Theatre wanted to lengthen Tom Thumb's engagement, but Barnum refused. He was playing for much larger stakes.

The methods he chose were methods that probably only Barnum would have imagined using and only Barnum could have made successful. From the first, Barnum was convinced that the only way to score a big success in England was to make Tom Thumb the darling of fashion. He reasoned that the common people would follow where the nobility led, and he cast about him for methods of inducing the nobility to see their duty and do it.

To introduce a midget from Bridgeport, Connecticut, into the highest and most exclusive circles of British society —and to make him positively the rage of that society— was no mean task, but it was to this that Barnum now set his hand. He began by renting from Lord Talbot a furnished mansion in Grafton Street in the exceedingly fashionable West End section of London. With only millionaires and lords of the realm for neighbors, Barnum now had a decidedly tony address from which to operate; and with typical Barnum brass, he began sending out invitations to editors and members of high society to come and see his "ward." Most of those invited came; all were much taken with Tom Thumb; and, as is the nature of man, those who had seen told those who hadn't and made them eager to see, too.

Soon lines of fine carriages ornamented with coats of arms were drawing up before the doors of the mansion in Grafton Street. Barnum now played a crafty game. He refused to admit even the highest lords of the realm to audience with Tom Thumb unless they had one of his special invitations. This put a premium on the invitations and spurred society gossip. Actually, of course, Barnum wasn't as exclusive as he pretended. His doorman had instructions to take the name and address of every caller who was turned away, and if the gentleman's lineage was sufficiently eminent, he was certain to get one of Barnum's now much-prized invitations to call the next day. By such devices, Barnum set a high premium on audiences with Tom Thumb without really offending anyone who mattered. Soon British society began to take the General at Barnum's high evaluation.

It was not long before Barnum and Tom Thumb crashed through the barrier into the high and haughty world that had seemed at first so inaccessible. One day an invitation arrived inviting them to appear that evening at the home of the Baroness Rothschild, the wife of the richest banker in London. The Baroness's mansion was in exclusive Piccadilly; and she sent her flashily decorated carriage, complete with driver and footman, to convey Barnum and Tom Thumb there.

That evening marked a new high point for the huge-framed showman from the little town of Bethel and the midget from Bridgeport, for the world they entered was one that outdazzled the wildest pictures their imaginations had painted. A cordon of liveried servants received them and escorted them into a brilliant hall, lined with statuary. They climbed a broad and impressive marble staircase, preceded by a liveried servant, and entered a huge room where the Baroness and a large party of guests were waiting for the General to entertain them. The Baroness was seated on a gorgeous couch, and around the room lords and ladies sat on chairs that looked to Barnum's dazed eyes as if they were made out of solid gold. Ebony, pearl, and gold practically blinded Barnum everywhere he looked. At the end of two hours, after Tom Thumb had captivated everybody, the two Yankees from rural Connecticut were escorted once more to the elegant coach to be driven home. But before they left, a servant sidled up to Barnum and pressed into his willing hands a fat purse loaded with gold.

Barnum's scheme was beginning to work. More invitations for private appearances at the homes of the wealthy followed; more fat purses chased each other along the path that the Baroness Rothschild's had taken into Barnum's capacious pockets. Barnum could probably have made a small fortune playing the nobility circuit, but he knew that there was a larger fortune to be reaped by getting the rich and titled to attract for him the shillings in the pockets of the multitude. And so he decided it was time to introduce Tom Thumb to the public of London. He engaged Egyptian Hall in Piccadilly and began to exhibit the General upon the stage. The elite flocked to these exhibitions, just as Barnum had hoped, and the populace, following where the elite led, began to pour out their shillings. The clink of hard coin sounded musically in Barnum's ears.

Still he was not completely satisfied. With Barnum, big triumphs only led to bigger, and he was never content until he had reaped the very biggest it was possible for him to imagine. One more thing was needed to send all London into a positive delirium over Tom Thumb, a reception by the Queen.

Barnum had had this in mind from the start; and, though such a thing had seemed impossible, he had never given up the hope of making the impossible come true. Horace Greeley, the great editor of the *Tribune* and a close friend, had given Barnum before he left New York a letter of introduction to Edward Everett, the United States Ambassador at the Court of St. James. Barnum and General Tom Thumb had dined with Everett, who was quite taken with them. And so it was through Everett that Barnum finally met Charles Murray, the Master of the Royal Household. Murray had written a book about a trip to America; Barnum had had the foresight to read the book, and he was diplomat enough to let Murray know how much he had admired it. This cemented relations. In a developing atmosphere of mutual admiration, Barnum found the opportunity to slip in a hint that he intended soon to take General Tom Thumb to Paris and present him to the French ruler, King Louis Philippe. The Master of the Royal Household rose to the bait; he felt certain that Queen Victoria would want to see the General before Louis

Philippe did. It was that simple. The invitation to Barnum and General Tom Thumb to appear at Buckingham Palace followed almost immediately.

On the night of their engagement with royalty, Barnum closed Egyptian Hall, posting on the outside of the door a card with a simple message worth a fortune. It read:

"Closed for the evening, General Tom Thumb being at Buckingham Palace by command of Her Majesty."

At the palace, before being admitted to the royal presence, Barnum was given precise instructions about his conduct. He must never speak to the Queen directly. If she asked him a question, it would be repeated to him by her Lord-in-Waiting; and he must answer through the Lord-in-Waiting, even though the Queen might be standing nearby in clear earshot. In leaving the Queen's presence, he must back out, bowing; he must never, in departing, turn his back upon Her Majesty. One of the lords of the household demonstrated the procedure by backing around an anteroom and having Barnum do the same. Once the official considered Barnum sufficiently schooled in these requirements of court etiquette, he and the general were led up a long marble staircase to the Queen's picture gallery, where Her Majesty, Prince Albert, the Duchess of Kent and about 20 of the high nobility were waiting.

Never had the big showman from Bethel and the knee-high midget from Bridgeport imagined a scene like this. There before them, in the magnificent picture gallery hung with priceless works of art, were the ladies of the court, dressed in the height of fashion, their gowns sparkling with diamonds, and there, in their midst stood

General Tom Thumb and Barnum amused Victoria's court no end.

Britain's most-beloved monarch, Queen Victoria herself. The Queen was not a large or impressive woman, and she was, as Barnum wrote, "modestly attired in plain black with no ornaments whatsoever." General Tom Thumb, strutting forward to meet the royal party, had some difficulty deciding which of the brilliantly dressed ladies might be the Queen; and so he halted in some confusion, bowed deeply and offered the only salutation he knew: "Good evening, Ladies and Gentlemen."

Since this was hardly the accepted way to address the Queen, everyone present laughed heartily at the midget's simplicity; but, with the kindness that was her strong trait of character, the Queen, that plain lady in black, quickly put him at his ease. Coming forward, she took his hand and led him around the picture gallery, describing the paintings to him and asking questions. When the tour ended, the little General, using an old Yankee expression, informed Her Majesty that her paintings were "first-rate." This drew another laugh, and then the General went into his act. He sangs his songs, did a dance or two, and went through his repertoire of impersonations. The royal party, just as common people everywhere had been, were fascinated by the wit and charm of this midget man.

Queen Victoria, curious to know more about the life of her tiny visitor, began to question Barnum. The Lord-in-Waiting, standing by her side, relayed her questions to Barnum, standing by *his* side; and when Barnum replied, he relayed Barnum's answers to the Queen, although Barnum and the Queen were standing so close together that each could hear the other perfectly. This silly rigamarole irritated the plain Yankee in Barnum; and after a few cumbersome questions and answers had been relayed in this fashion, he pitched etiquette overboard and replied to the Queen directly. The Lord-in-Waiting was horrified; the court circle gasped. But the heavens did not fall. Indeed, the Queen herself smiled, as if to say that she was weary, too, of such conversation through a go-between; and from that moment she and the onetime storekeeper from Bethel chatted with a "total absence of formality."

Finally, it came time to leave, and Barnum began to execute the difficult backward step and bow he had been taught. General Tom Thumb imitated him perfectly, and for a few seconds all went well. But there is a great difference between the backward step of a man six feet two and the backward step of one who is only two feet. Tom Thumb, darting a swift glance around him, saw that he was being rapidly outdistanced in the retreat to the door. What was he to do? He took a look at the royal group, another glance at Barnum, and then he turned and scampered to catch up. Reaching Barnum, he whirled around and began once more his backing and bowing. The court circle was convulsed with laughter, and the excitement communicated itself to the Queen's pet poodle who, unwilling to overlook such a breach of manners, angrily charged the General. Tom Thumb was startled by this attack by an animal almost as large as he was; and, grabbing his tiny cane, he flailed away at the ferocious poodle, then turned and ran once more to catch up with Barnum, whirled and began backing again, striking at the poodle as he backed. And so, wafted on a gale of laughter that probably had never been surpassed in court history, the two Yankees made their unprecedented exit from the royal presence.

With this reception at Buckingham Palace, the European tour of Barnum and Tom Thumb became virtually assured of success. Once England's beloved Queen had received "the least of the little men," hardly any man who called himself an Englishman could rest content until he, too, had seen this smallest of nature's wonders. Barnum doubtless could have reaped a fortune by relying on the prestige this court reception gave him; but, being Barnum, he overlooked no opportunity and spared no expense to make the British public even more conscious of Tom Thumb than it already was.

Determined to keep his little man constantly in the public eye, Barnum went to the carriage maker who built conveyances for the Queen and commissioned him to build a tiny carriage especially proportioned for Tom Thumb. The resulting equipeage had a body only a foot wide and 20 inches high, but no detail was spared to make it as showy as the gaudiest carriage of any lord of the realm. The interior was finished in elegant style, lined with beautifully figured yellow silk, and equipped with plate glass windows that opened and shut at the touch of a spring. The outside of the body was painted an intense blue, trimmed with crimson and white, good patriotic American colors, and the wheels were blue and red with silver hub caps. Barnum even invented a coat of arms for the General and had it painted on the doors. It consisted of the figures of Britannia and the Goddess of Liberty, supported by the British lion and the American eagle, with the crest the rising sun shining on the British and American flags, and underneath the legend, "Go Ahead!" Barnum hunted the British Isles to find appropriate horsepower for this diminutive carriage, and he finally found what he sought, a pair of small Shetland ponies standing only 34 inches high. When these ponies had been harnessed to the carriage, when a dwarf whom Barnum engaged as a driver had mounted the box in front, and another serving as a footman rode on the step behind, Tom Thumb was ready to take a spin through the streets of London in style. Needless to say, he and his carriage and his stunted ponies and his dwarf retainers made a sight such as no Londoner had ever seen before— a sight that could not fail to arouse curiosity and stimulate attendance at Egyptian Hall.

Tom Thumb now became the greatest attraction of his day. Twice more, Queen Victoria summoned him and Barnum back to Buckingham Palace to entertain the royal circle. Each time, Tom Thumb worked his enchantment on everyone. Introduced to the Prince of Wales, he looked up at the normally tall youth and remarked: "The Prince is taller than I am, but I *feel* as big as anybody." Then he proceeded to strut up and down the room, his chest puffed out in mock pride, while the court laughed. Introduced to the Princess Royal, the General led her to a miniature sofa that Barnum had brought along and sat chatting with her, just like a boy and girl back in Bridgeport. On one of these visits, asked by the Queen to sing his favorite song, General Tom Thumb, with charming impudence, broke out into "Yankee Doodle"; and the Queen, with admirable good humor, pronounced this tune of the revolution that had cost her country most of its American empire a mighty fine song indeed. So charmed was Queen Victoria by the antics of Tom Thumb that she had an elaborate souvenir made for him, an ornament of mother-of-pearl set in emeralds.

"I am very much obliged," Tom Thumb told her. "I shall keep it as long as I live."

These court appearances, with Barnum doing the masterminding, were well publicized throughout all of Britain, and there is little wonder that, under the circumstances, Egyptian Hall became so crowded that Barnum had to rent larger quarters to display his prize, half-pint attraction. For several months, the General drew an audience of 2,000 persons a day; and frequently as many as 50 or 60 carriages, many of them boasting noble coats of arms, would be lined up waiting in the street before his exhibition hall. Among the famous who came to see him was Britain's greatest soldier, the Duke of Wellington, the conqueror of Napoleon at the Battle of Waterloo. As it happened, just as the Duke entered the hall, Tom Thumb was in the middle of his impersonation of Napoleon, striding up and down the platform, head bowed on stuck-out chest.

When Barnum stopped the general in his moody pacing and introduced him to the Duke, the latter asked what he had been thinking while he was impersonating Napoleon.

Quick as a flash came the answer:

"I was thinking about the loss of the Battle of Waterloo."

The Duke of Wellington laughed heartily at the witty reply; so did all who heard it; and the story soon was told over all of England.

When even Tom Thumb's drawing power in London eventually began to wane, Barnum took him on the long-contemplated tour of France. Triumph now led to triumph; one triumph built upon the triumph that had gone before, and each new triumph fed a future one. With the much-publicized conquest of the British Isles behind him, Tom Thumb's conquest of France was virtually assured. He was invited to the Tuileries by the gay king, Louis Philippe, and he charmed the French court as he had charmed the British court before it. As in England, he played to packed houses. Seats were sold out for two months in advance; Barnum's profits were so burdensome that, each night, he had to hire a cab in which to cart them home. Valuable gifts were showered on Tom Thumb and Barnum by the pleasure-loving French court. In the provinces, in every city Tom Thumb visited, the public flocked to see him, and Barnum repeated his endless golden triumphs.

The success in France was the platform on which Barnum built a triumphal tour of Europe. In Spain, General Tom Thumb was received by Queen Isabella and attended a bull fight. In Brussels, he spent a day at the palace of King Leopold and entertained the children of the Belgian royal family. Returning to London, he played a return engagement; and, just as his previous English triumph had stimulated his continental triumphs, so now his continental triumphs whetted the desire of the British public to see him all over again. The crowds surpassed those he had drawn before, and the receipts were fatter even than they had been during his first appearance.

Barnum, seeing that the love affair of Tom Thumb

[*113*]

and his European audiences was likely to be of years-long duration, returned to New York in October, 1844, leaving the management of the General in the hands of his father. Taking Charity and his daughters back to London with him, Barnum went on tour with the General through England, Scotland and Ireland, then revisited the continent. Everywhere they went, Tom Thumb continued to harvest a gold mine. After the first year, Barnum took the little General into full partnership, and for the next two years they split the profits equally. There were certainly profits enough to split. When Barnum and Tom Thumb finally returned to the United States after three years of unrivaled success, a British newspaper reported that they had harvested some 150,000 British pounds, about $750,000 in American money, a truly fantastic sum in a day when the dollar was worth several times as much as it is now.

It was in February, 1847, that Barnum and his petite attraction returned to New York. Once more past triumphs insured future ones. Tom Thumb, the mite from Bridgeport whom Barnum originally had billed as an English celebrity, now deserved the title; and all New York flocked to see the little man who had never failed to charm both the European commoner and the European king and queen. The American Museum had never seen such crowds as Tom Thumb now drew; and when Barnum finally took his minute and witty actor on tour, in all America it was the same. In Washington, Barnum and his midget general were received at the White House by President and Mrs. Polk. In Philadelphia, they took in $5,594.91 in twelve days; in the cities of the South and in Havana, Cuba, crowds poured a golden stream into the Barnum-Tom Thumb treasury. For the entire tour, receipts averaged more than $500 a day, expenses only $25—a disparity that warmed the cockles of Barnum's heart.

Tom Thumb, for Barnum, was a living, performing, veritable gold mine, an attraction that opened the gateway to colossal fortune and that seemed to have no end. Barnum was not exaggerating when, on one occasion, he pointed to the General and exclaimed:

"That is my piece of goods; I have sold it hundreds of thousands of times and never delivered it!"

Chapter **8**

Jenny Lind

P hineas T. Barnum, back in the United States with the gold of Europe in his pockets, found himself a man of great wealth. He was 46 years old; the American Museum was a never-failing gold mine; and Tom Thumb, on tour of the hinterlands, was making money almost as fast as the U.S. Mint. With such resources and such prospects, Barnum decided that it was time for him to establish himself and his family in a permanent home that would do credit to his acquired status.

Both he and Charity, natives of the Nutmeg state, decided that only Connecticut would do. Bridgeport appealed to Barnum. It was on Long Island Sound, with a beautiful view across the water; and it was linked by railroad to nearby New York, where Barnum's business constantly called him. Barnum purchased 17 acres of land a mile from the center of the town and began to build.

He knew exactly the kind of a mansion he wanted— an Oriental castle that would catch the eyes of all beholders and would be in itself a unique tribute to showmanship. While in England, Barnum had been greatly impressed by Brighton Pavilion, built by Queen Victoria's uncle, George IV. The pavilion was studded with spires and minarets, and was representative of the gingerbread architecture of the Victorian era. Barnum, much impressed, had commissioned a British architect to draw plans along similar lines for the home that he intended to construct in America.

The result was a baroque palace that Barnum named Iranistan. It was three stories high, with broad piazzas and large, arched window-ways. It was a jumble of Byzantine, Moorish, and Turkish architecture. Minarets and spires stuck up all over the place in grotesque confusion. At either end of the building were large, domed conservatories. The Oriental atmosphere of the exterior was matched by the Oriental splendor of the interior. A large winding staircase, patterned no doubt after those of the Baroness Rothschild and Queen Victoria that had so impressed Barnum, led upward from the main hall and was lined with marble statuary. The panels of the drawing-room walls were painted with scenes to represent the four seasons. Pier glasses and mirrored folding doors added to its glamor. In the dining room, rich wall panels represented Music, Painting, and Poetry. Adjoining the dining room was a Chinese library, with Chinese landscapes in oils and Chinese furniture. The walls in Barnum's private study were brocaded in a rich orange satin, and adjoining the study was a bathroom, with a shower of hot and cold water. A New York visitor, struck speechless by such splendor, could only compare the interior of Barnum's castle with the most gaudily decorated object of the day; it was, he wrote, "as elegant as a steamboat."

In all of this, Barnum had a purpose. He didn't want just a home; he didn't want just to show off; he wanted both a home and an advertisement. He wrote that he thought "a pile of buildings of a novel order might indirectly serve as an advertisement of my various enterprises." Iranistan was fashioned with that end in mind. A large iron fence surrounded its broad acres; fountains were scattered about in lavish profusion; through the park, elk and reindeer roamed. Since the tracks of the New York & New Haven Railroad passed close by, Barnum had a daily, changing audience whom he could impress with his deliberate extravagance and splendor. Certainly, no one could whirl past Iranistan on the railroad without being startled by the Far Eastern minarets and spires that poked up from the Connecticut countryside; and certainly no one, so startled, would be so incurious as not to want to know the name of the owner of this weird and splendid mansion.

Barnum and his family moved into Iranistan in November, 1848, and shortly afterwards gave a housewarming for 1,000 guests. Now began a new period in his career. He became a local celebrity. He was now more than just a tricky showman; he was also a landed country gentleman with status to maintain. He became president of the Fairfield County Agricultural Society, president of the Pequennock Bank. With these new titles symbolizing his new distinction, Barnum, often called the Prince of Humbug, began to take a more serious and responsible view of life.

For one thing, he became a Prohibitionist.

Drinking was one of the great vices of early America. In colonial days, it was common practice to get breakfast under way with a tankard of ale—and to go on from there. Temperance was for generations an art practically unknown, and the drunkard was the cross borne by a hard-drinking society. Barnum had been shocked by the evil of drink for the first time in 1847 when he went to Saratoga Springs to manage Tom Thumb's appearance at the New York State Fair. Here he saw so many New Yorkers of wealth and distinction so completely inebriated that he was jolted into some sharp and searching self-examination.

In show business, he had to meet people every day, and it was a common practice to take a few drinks with them. Barnum had not worried about it until he was suddenly confronted with the spectacle of so many eminent New Yorkers staggering around him at Saratoga. Then he thought: "What guarantee is there that I may not become a drunkard?" He shuddered at the prospect and swore off strong liquors. He still maintained a well-stocked wine cellar at Iranistan, consoling himself for a time with the thought that wine wasn't really such a menace; but one night he heard a minister, a personal friend of his, give such a fiery temperance speech that he went home so worried he could not sleep. Even wine, he realized, might set him on the path of downfall; and, rising in the night, he went down into the Iranistan cellar and knocked the heads off all his champagne bottles. Returning upstairs, he told Charity what he had done, and she wept with relief and joy.

[*119*]

Having by this decisive action demonstrated to himself that he was a strong character, Barnum embarked on a campaign to stiffen the spines of his suffering fellow men. He began to make speeches, he began to write articles on the evils of the Demon Rum. In one statement of Prohibitionist views, he wrote: "We had become convinced that it was a matter of life and death; that we must *kill* Alcohol, or Alcohol would kill *us*, or our friends."

This moral crusade of Barnum's led him to a novel experiment on the stage of his American Museum. During his proprietorship of the Museum, he had greatly enlarged the original Lecture Room until, in its stage and seating arrangements, it was as fine as any theater in New York. On this stage, Barnum now presented *The Moral, Domestic Drama of The Drunkard, or The Fallen Saved.* This five-act play traced the downfall of a drunkard, the embarrassment and impoverishment of his family, his "despair and attempted suicide," and final salvation when he is induced by "a Temperance philanthropist" to give up the evil of liquor. After each performance, it was announced from the stage that any who wished to sign the pledge and become a teetotaler might do so at the box office. Such was the effect, Barnum wrote, that "almost every hour during the day and evening women could be seen bringing their husbands to the Museum to sign the pledge." The reception New York gave Barnum's morality play on the evils of liquor was astounding. The drama was performed nightly and regularly drew from 2,000 to 3,000 persons; it ran through several hundred performances and was so successful that other New York theaters felt compelled to imitate and broke out into a rash of dramas on the theme of *The Drunkard*. Horace Greeley in the *Tribune* crowed with delight, and editorially gave Barnum credit for elevating the moral tone of the theater.

By such stages had Barnum, the exhibitor of freaks, turned into Barnum, the uplifter of moral standards. He had achieved a station in life; he had a certain dignity to maintain; and in the fall of 1849, while resting at Iranistan, his mind was busy with a variety of new projects that would be, not just beneficial to his pocketbook, but flattering to his reputation. He toyed with the idea of a Congress of Nations, an exhibition that would result from a worldwide hunt for the perfect man and woman. He actually sent an agent abroad to study the various types of humanity that might be exhibited in this search for perfection. But, while this groundwork was being done, Barnum's fertile imagination gave birth to a new and more exciting project—Jenny Lind.

Jenny Lind was at this moment, in October, 1849, the most famous singer in the world. Throughout Europe, she was known as The Swedish Nightingale. She was the improbable daughter of an improbable union—her father, a ne'er-do-well roisterer, her mother, pious, strict narrow-minded, stubborn. As a little girl, the only affection Jenny Lind knew she received from a grandmother, who lived in a home for widows and with whom she stayed most of the time. When Jenny was only nine years old, she was singing a song one day to a pet cat. The maid of a dancer at the Royal Opera House happened to overhear her and told her mistress of the girl with a golden voice.

"A small, ugly, broad-nosed, shy, gauche and under-grown girl," as Jenny later described herself, she was brought before the singing master of the Royal Theater. This august person at first felt insulted to be asked to listen to such a child; but when he heard her sing, he wept in his excitement and made arrangements to have her brought up at the expense of the government and given vocal training. At the age of 10, she first appeared upon the stage of the Royal Theater. About the same time, she began singing in private concerts; and when she was 17, she made her debut in opera and at once scored a triumph. By the time she was 20, she was the idol of Sweden as both an actress and a singer.

She was offered a long contract with the Royal Theater, but she refused it and, at 21, went to Paris for further voice training. She was no longer small or shy or under-grown. She was never to be beautiful, but she possessed a well-rounded figure; she had wholesome and attractive features; and when she sang, her face became lighted by some magical inner radiance that brought audiences wor-shipping at her feet.

Despite the eminence she had achieved at an extremely early age, she possessed a deeply religious vein and, like her mother, a kind of moral severity. Paris, with its license, its love of pleasure, disgusted her; and she resolved never to sing there. When her training was finished, she re-turned to Sweden, a more accomplished artist than she had been when she left it; and in the next two years, she became the rage of both Sweden and Denmark. These triumphs prepared the way for others. She went to Germany; she sang in Berlin; and soon the Germans, like the Danes and the Swedes, were her slaves. In Vienna, world capital of music, she was called before the curtain 25 times and the Empress Mother of Austria dropped a wreath at her feet. Thousands waited in the streets until daybreak for her to leave the opera house; and when at last she did, enthusiastic students unharnessed the horses from her carriage, and a detachment of cavalry was needed to get her back to her lodgings.

After these triumphs on the continent, Jenny Lind went to England in the spring of 1847. She arrived just a few months after Barnum and Tom Thumb had departed; and so it happened that Barnum had never met her, had never heard her sing. But he knew, from reading British newspapers and periodicals, that she had repeated in England all of her earlier, tremendous successes, and he thought: if in England, why not America? Why not, indeed! He would bring Jenny Lind to the United States!

It would be difficult to imagine a less likely project for profit. Americans were definitely not a music loving people. Though Jenny Lind was The Swedish Nightingale and the heroine of Europe, the possessor of a voice (according to her legion of admirers) such as the world had never heard before, Americans as a people had never heard of Jenny Lind. Only a few in musical circles, only those rare individuals who read the European newspapers were even aware that such a person as Jenny Lind existed. Just how Barnum came to imagine that even he could make unmusical America swoon at the feet of Jenny Lind is something that he never fully explained. He wrote only that, after the idea came to him, he spent several days at Iranistan making calculations on the backs of old envelopes and pieces of scrap paper; and each time he figured up the potential cost and the potential profit, he came out with a fat, juicy, Barnum-sized gain.

All this figuring and refiguring led Barnum to two conclusions: "1st. The chances were greatly in favor of an immense pecuniary success; and 2nd. Inasmuch as my name has long been associated with 'humbug,' and the American public suspect that my capacities do not extend beyond the power to exhibit a stuffed monkey-skin or a dead mermaid, I can afford to lose fifty thousand dollars in such an enterprise as bringing to this country, in the zenith of her life and celebrity, the greatest musical wonder in the world, provided the engagement is carried out with credit to the management."

Ten years earlier, Barnum would not have worried about that "credit to the management," but now credit was becoming almost as important as cash in his life. Like many another man before and since, having acquired great wealth with a strong assist from trickery and engaging roguery, he now wanted to gild his money with the respectability of good works. It was worth to him even the possible loss of $50,000; and so he hunted out John Hall Wilton, an English musician then on tour in America, and sent him to Europe to get Jenny Lind's signature on a contract.

Wilton sailed on November 6, 1849, carrying letters of instruction from Barnum and letters of introduction to Barnum's bankers, Baring Brothers in London. When Wilton arrived, he learned that Jenny Lind was in Lubeck, Germany, resting after a concert tour. She already had had other offers to make a tour of America, and she had turned them all down. She later disclosed that two things about Barnum impressed her from the start. First, he was the only promoter who did not ask her to assume the risk of losses while holding out to her the lure of profits. Second, she was much impressed by the picture of Iranistan on Barnum's letterhead. After she finally came to America and stayed at Iranistan, she told Barnum: "Do you know, Mr. Barnum, if you had not built Iranistan, I should never have come to America for you?" She explained that she had not wanted to undertake the long ocean voyage, she was homesick for Sweden, and she had been tempted to say "no" to Barnum as she had to all others. But the picture of Iranistan arrested her attention. "I said to myself," she told Barnum, "a gentleman who has been so successful in his business as to be able to build and reside in such as place cannot be a mere 'adventurer.' So I wrote to your agent, and consented to an interview, which I should have declined if I had not seen the picture of Iranistan."

Once more, Barnum's instinct for showmanship had proved itself infallible; he had intended that Iranistan should advertise him. It had. And it had recommended him, too, to The Swedish Nightingale, whom others had found unapproachable.

With the picture of Iranistan before her as visual proof of Barnum's wealth, Jenny Lind set herself the pleasurable task of carving out a slice of the showman's fortune. She wanted money, not so much for herself, but to endow a hospital for poor children in Stockholm; and the contract that was drawn up with Barnum provided plenty both for herself and the hospital. Under its terms, Jenny Lind was to sing 150 concerts a year under Barnum's management at $1,000 a concert. He was to pay all her expenses; he was to pay the salaries and expenses of her accompanist and musical director; and, what is more, he was to deposit in cash with her bankers in Europe the full amount of the money guaranteed her before she sailed. The sum came to $187,500. And Barnum did not have $187,500 lying around in cash.

He tried desperately to raise the money, but Wall Street bankers laughed at him. They told him bluntly that his lavish Jenny Lind contract would ruin him. This only made Barnum the more determined to succeed. He mortgaged all his property to the hilt, and by this means raised all but $5,000. That last $5,000 seemed a stumbling block, but finally a good friend, one of the leading Universalist preachers in the nation, made him the loan. Barnum deposited the $187,500 to Jenny Lind's credit in Europe. It was certain now: The Swedish Nightingale would come to America.

Barnum had hoped to keep word of his Jenny Lind negotiations secret until he could promote them as he wished, but rumors leaked out and were printed in the press. Reading the stories one day while he was traveling by train from Philadelphia to New York, Barnum decided to conduct an on-the-spot test of public sentiment. Engaging the conductor in conversation, Barnum told him that he had just hired Jenny Lind. The conductor looked puzzled.

"Jenny Lind?" he asked. "Is she a dancer?"

The question shocked Barnum. If even a conductor, a man in constant touch with people and affairs, did not have the foggiest notion who Jenny Lind was, how was the great American public to be made so conscious of her and her talents that it would flock to her concerts? Just by asking himself that question, Barnum could see the enormity of the task before him.

He had some six months in which to work on the American mind before Jenny Lind arrived, and never did a promoter work harder. Jenny Lind was giving a last series of concerts in England, and Barnum hired a music critic to write glowing accounts of them for a Liverpool newspaper. The concerts were a series of frenzied triumphs; the British newspaper accounts were almost as frenzied; and Barnum, with his newspaper friends, saw to it that the British notices were prominently displayed in the New York press. Such was the beginning of the American public's education about Jenny Lind. But with Barnum working behind the scenes, it was only the beginning.

In his official announcement that he had hired Jenny Lind and was bringing her to America, he set out deliberately to create an image. He wrote grandly that he would have brought Jenny Lind to America even though he knew he would "not make a farthing profit," so anxious was he for Americans to have the privilege of seeing "a lady whose vocal powers have never been approached by any other human being, and whose character is charity, simplicity and goodness personified." Barnum loved superlatives. Whatever he was exhibiting was always the oddest or the smallest or the best, and with Jenny Lind he set out to create a double image—the best and the purest. Barnum laid heavy emphasis on her character, her deeply religious streak, her intense interest in charity, that hospital for the poor children of Stockholm that her concerts would endow. He later wrote in his autobiography that he never would have signed the contract with Jenny Lind except for this aspect of her character. He felt that her "extraordinary benevolence and generosity" would attract the American public at least as much as her singing and that "there were multitudes of individuals in America who would be prompted to attend her concerts by this feeling alone." In all his publicity Barnum sought to convince the American public that they were going to have the privilege, not only of listening to the greatest voice in the world, but of seeing a virtual saint. He was billing a two-in-one, lifetime attraction. And he billed it in every manner his clever mind could devise.

Meeting an English newspaperman who had seen Jenny Lind and heard her sing, Barnum hired him to write a series of glowing articles to appear once or twice each week, describing Jenny Lind's admirable character, the glories of her voice, the tremendous receptions she had received in Europe. The articles were all datelined London and appeared in American newspapers under the guise of special correspondence from that city. They kept running until even Barnum ran out of ideas about how to give a new appearance to details that had been printed many times over. "I suppose that was the first attempt in this country to 'work the press,'" Barnum later confessed. Whether it was the first or not, Barnum did indeed work it well.

He always had some new gimmick up his sleeve. In addition to the glowing articles about Jenny Lind that he was pumping into the columns of the newspapers, he decided to whip up public interest by holding a contest. The seed was planted in a letter that he had Jenny Lind's musical director, Julius Benedict, write to the New York newspapers. In this, Benedict pronounced Jenny's voice more glorious than ever after her rest in Germany; and he just happened to remark that she would like to sing a new, special song of welcome to America at her first concert in the New World.

This was Barnum's cue. He advertised that, since Jenny Lind had said she wanted a new song, he would pay $200 for an original poem that could be set to music for her first performance. The contest stirred wide interest, as contests always do, and 753 poems were submitted. The judges finally selected one by Bayard Taylor, a prominent poet and writer of the day. It was not a particularly good poem; the 752 poets who had lost all were miffed; and there was a long and heated controversy over the management of the poetry contest. All of this, naturally, pleased Barnum; brickbats as well as bouquets were grist for his publicity mill. He welcomed them all.

In his autobiography, he even chuckled at a witty pamphlet that was published at this time attacking his poetry contest and his management of the Jenny Lind enterprise. The pamphlet contained a number of poems that, Barnum conceded, "gave some capital hits." One poet, after describing the freaks in Barnum's Museum, pictured

[*129*]

him as still seeking additional novelties and speaking to
The Swedish Nightingale as his latest find in this vein:

"So, Jenny, come along! you're just the card for me,
"And quit these kings and queens, for the country of
the free;
"They'll welcome you with speeches, and serenades,
and rockets,
"And you will touch their hearts, and I will tap their
pockets;
"And if between us both the public isn't skinned,
"Why, my name isn't Barnum, nor your name Jenny
Lind!"

The poet was a true prophet. With the sailing of
Jenny Lind for America, the popular frenzy that Barnum
had whipped up rose to a peak that seems almost unbeliev-
able today. Jenny left England on the steamer *Atlantic*,
which the press promptly dubbed "the Jenny Lind Boat."
Every berth on board was taken by passengers avid to sail
with her, anxious to get a glimpse of her; and on each of
the 11 days that it took the liner to cross the ocean, items
appeared in the New York press about its progress and the
ever nearer approach of the divine singer, who was about
to honor America with her presence.

The buildup was perfect in its artistry. By the time
the *Atlantic* neared American shores, all New York was
agog for the sight of Jenny Lind. The arrival was a master-
piece of timing. The liner broke out of the ocean mists and
came up the harbor on a Sunday morning, September 1,
1850, and the populace of the city, taking their leisure on
this nonworking day, turned out virtually en masse to get

a glimpse of the celebrity about whom, by now, it had heard so much.

Barnum went down the harbor to meet the *Atlantic*, boarded the vessel with a large bouquet in his hands, and so met and talked for the first time with the singer on whom he had risked his entire fortune. He had no doubts, for the magic of publicity was working for him. As the ship came up the harbor, whistles, foghorns, bells, everything that would make a noise gave voice; and in a perfect hurricane of sound, the vessel was warped into her slip at Canal Street. There some 30,000 screaming, waving New Yorkers had assembled. West Street for a dozen blocks was clogged by the crowd; and when the ship drew near the wharf, the mob surged forward with such force that one man in the front row lost his balance and pitched headlong into the water.

After he had been rescued, after the vessel had been made fast, more mob scenes followed. Barnum had gone to considerable trouble and expense to create the impression that the city itself was giving Jenny an official welcome, and the huge crowd added to this impression. Across the dock, Barnum's workmen had erected two huge triumphal arches made of trees and flowers and decorated with flags. On one an inscription read: "Welcome, Jenny Lind!" On the other, "Welcome to America!" The gangplank had been specially carpeted. When Jenny appeared and began to descend, the enthusiasm of the crowd burst all bounds.

Dock gates crashed before the rush; men and women were trampled underfoot and injured. Strong lines of police formed to protect The Swedish Nightingale, and they had

[*131*]

their hands full forcing a path for her through the throng to the street where Barnum's carriage waited. As she seated herself in the coach, some of Barnum's employees, stationed nearby for the purpose, hurled bouquets of flowers through the windows onto her lap in what was made to appear a spontaneous gesture of public affection. Doubtless, Jenny thought it was; probably the crowd itself thought it was. But actually it was all the work of Barnum, who mounted now to the box beside the driver to make certain by his well-known presence that everyone in New York should realize *this* was "the Jenny Lind carriage."

Everywhere along the streets, people saw the carriage and recognized the huge figure of Barnum upon the box— and knew that Jenny Lind at last had arrived. The crowd hemmed in the carriage, followed it, blocked its way. Only with the greatest difficulty could a path be forced through streets clogged with admirers of Jenny Lind, and it was after three o'clock in the afternoon before the party reached the Irving House on Broadway, where Barnum had engaged rooms. Some 5,000 persons were already waiting in front of the hotel; and before many minutes had passed, the crowd had swelled to 10,000.

Even after the Nightingale had disappeared inside, the crowd lingered and, if anything, grew. All through the afternoon, all through the evening, it stayed. Everytime a shadow passed in front of a lighted window in Jenny Lind's suite, a shout would go up. Half an hour after midnight there came a new demonstration. The New York Musical Fund Society, its musicians escorted by 300 firemen carrying torches, came marching down Broadway and halted in front of the hotel to serenade Jenny. Some 20,000 spectators cheered. Broadway was completely blocked. Sightseers lined the rooftops, clustered in the windows of neighboring buildings, even climbed and clung to the lamp posts.

Barnum, wooing the favor of the throng, led Jenny Lind out to one of the hotel balconies. He asked the musicians to play "Yankee Doodle" and "Hail, Columbia," and Jenny Lind waved to the crowd and applauded both songs. The crowd waved back and cheered and went almost out of its mind. Not until almost dawn did it finally disperse and let Jenny get some sleep.

This first mad fever of welcome was only a symptom of the fever that was to come. Barnum, with his wily use of publicity, had wrought so well that Jenny Lind could not set foot outside her hotel without being almost mobbed by well-wishers. Everywhere she went, she was followed, admired, adored. It became obvious to Barnum that not even the largest hall in New York would be too large for Jenny Lind's concerts; and so he rented the largest place he could find, the great, circular Castle Garden, originally built as a fort at the tip of Manhattan Island, in later years to see long service as the city's aquarium, and capable of accommodating, both sitting and standing, some 10,000 persons.

With the fever to see and hear Jenny Lind raging through the veins of New Yorkers, Barnum now calculated that, for The Swedish Nightingale's first appearance, he could not only fill Castle Garden—but he could fill it at a premium. And so he decided to hold an auction, selling tickets for choice seats to the highest bidders. The auction

[*133*]

drew a crowd of 4,000 persons, and bidding for the honor of buying the first ticket was frantic. A hatter by the name of Genin, whose store adjoined Barnum's Museum, finally copped the prize, paying $225 for the first ticket to the first Jenny Lind concert. It was an incredible price, in those days, but it was the best investment Genin ever made. Newspapers throughout the nation carried stories about Genin, the hatter. Millions of persons who had never known Genin existed knew about him now; customers mobbed his shop; and, as Barnum wrote, Genin, by paying $225 for a ticket to hear Jenny Lind, "laid the foundation of his fortune."

Genin had plenty of company in paying extravagant prices for tickets to the first Jenny Lind concert. It took two days to auction off all the seats in Castle Garden. When the last ticket had been sold, Barnum counted a take of $17,864.05. It was incredible—and to listen to a singer, at that! Barnum now had only one worry. Had the expectations of the public been built too high? Could even Jenny Lind live up to them? Or would she prove a crashing disappointment?

The answer was given on the night of September 11, 1850, when Jenny, clad in a dress of virginal white, walked gracefully down between the music stands, escorted by Julius Benedict, and faced an audience that practically hung from the rafters of Castle Garden. Outside on the river, close under the walls of the old fort, more than 200 boats lay at anchor, carrying more than a thousand persons anxious to get close enough to hear the notes of that marvelous voice. They waited not knowing, of course, what was happening when, inside the hall, the mere appearance of The Swedish Nightingale touched off pandemonium. The immense crowd rose to its feet, applauding, shouting, screaming, throwing things. Jenny curtsied deeply, a gesture of grace that only made the riot more riotous. Startled, fearful, she gazed out upon the mad scene, and when enough quiet had been restored so that she could begin to sing, she seemed shaken by the experience. Her voice wavered uncertainly, and for a fearful moment, it seemed she might break down completely.

But then she regained her confidence and self-possession. The clear, sweet notes of the voice that never failed to send music critics into raptures swelled out through the hall; and when she finished her first song, the stage was showered with bouquets, handkerchiefs waved, and men shouted hoarsely. The storm of enthusiasm inside was equalled by the storm of enthusiasm outside. Those listening in the boats were possessed of a frantic desire to get into the hall, and they tried to land on the water side of the castle and break their way in. Police met them and drove them back with much shouting and brandishing of clubs; and through all the tumult, Jenny Lind kept singing, piece after piece, each song leaving her audience more enraptured than the song before.

At the close of the concert, there were loud cries of "Barnum! Barnum!" and Barnum himself, the man who had made it all possible, "reluctantly" (in his own words) appeared upon the stage. There he led an adoring city in praise of Jenny Lind. She hadn't wanted him to say anything about it, he informed the audience, but actually The

Swedish Nightingale, out of the generosity of her own heart, was donating all of her profits from this night's performance to New York charities. Barnum read off a long list of organizations Jenny Lind was helping, and once more New

The audience in Castle Garden went wild when Jenny Lind sang.

Yorkers went wild. They were convinced both that they had been privileged to listen to a great voice and to see an exceptionally noble woman.

Such was the thunderous debut that made Jenny Lind the talk of all America. There was no question that her success—and Barnum's—would be great. The only question was: How great? The public quickly gave the answer. In six concerts in New York, Barnum collected $87,055.89. Then he took Jenny Lind on to Boston, to Philadelphia, and Baltimore and Washington. Everywhere they went, Jenny was received by the most distinguished Americans of the day; everywhere they went, Jenny drew huge and enthusiastic crowds and sang to huge and well-paying audiences. The tour continued into 1851 with unabated success. In May, Barnum and Jenny Lind returned to New York and gave 14 more concerts. The financial rewards were enormous, but behind the scenes trouble was brewing.

Some of Jenny Lind's European advisers were jealous of Barnum. Although Barnum had rewritten the terms of the original contract and split all profits with Jenny after a minimum guarantee to himself, although he paid all the expenses and assumed all the risks, some of Jenny's intimates kept insisting that he was making too much money out of her talents. There was, in addition, another cause of friction. Julius Benedict, in poor health, had been forced to return to Europe, and he had been replaced by Otto Goldschmidt, a cold and exacting young German musician with whom Jenny Lind soon fell in love. Probably no two men could ever have been found who were more unlike each other, more certain to rub each other the wrong way, than Barnum and Goldschmidt. The cold, withdrawing Goldschmidt and the bubbling, zestful Barnum simply were not made to get along together. And Jenny Lind loved Goldschmidt.

This mere fact made a break inevitable. The dissension that had been brewing for months finally came to a head during a return engagement in Philadelphia. Barnum had booked three concerts in the National Theater, which had been used recently for a circus. The dressing room still smelled like a stable; and Jenny Lind, in a gust of anger, informed Barnum that *she* was not a horse.

It was an angry outburst that brought all the bickerings of months into the open. Even Barnum's nerves were frayed at the necessity of presenting constantly to the public an unwavering image of sweetness and light when, in reality, behind the scene, sweetness and light were swiftly vanishing conditions. So, when Jenny Lind offered to pay Barnum a $32,000 forfeit to break her contract, he agreed.

Their partnership was terminated after nine months and 93 concerts. For both, it had been a fantastically successful arrangement. They had grossed the incredible sum of $712,161.34. Even after deducting the $32,000 she paid Barnum to break the contract, Jenny Lind had a net profit of $176,675.09 for nine months work, a fabulous sum in an age in which there was no income tax and the dollar was worth its weight in gold. Barnum's own gross came to $534,486.25. He never revealed how much of this was clear profit; but, even assuming that his expenses exceeded $300,000, this still would have left him with some $200,000, a sum more than ample to finance a brief period of rest and recuperation among the domes and spires of Iranistan.

Barnum could afford to let Jenny Lind go, but she could less afford to be without the services of Barnum. She continued to give concerts, but almost from the moment that she and Barnum parted, these were less successful financially than they had been. The novelty of Jenny Lind was wearing off with the American public, and there was no Barnum there to keep her "angel side" always turned to the public, to keep freshening and restoring the image. On the contrary, Goldschmidt, whom Jenny soon married, seems to have impressed Americans as cold and unsympathetic. He was in addition a routine musician, and applause for him was sometimes so exaggerated as to sound like boos. Attendance fell off. When Jenny Lind held her farewell concert in Castle Garden on May 24, 1852, the hall was not crowded and receipts were only some $7,000, far less than half of what they had been for that first performance under Barnum's direction. Yet anyone, knowing what Barnum had done with Tom Thumb's farewell to the American public just before he had sailed for England, can easily imagine what enthusiasm Barnum would have whipped up for "this positively last appearance" of the glorious Swedish Nightingale. In the sharp contrast shines the genius of Barnum.

Jenny Lind, back in Europe, soon went into lifelong retirement. She preferred the role of Mrs. Otto Goldschmidt, housewife, to that of Jenny Lind, The Swedish Nightingale. Her new role, except for brief appearances for charity, she maintained to the end of her life. As for Barnum, he had accomplished the inconceivable by his Jenny Lind promotion. He had not only made a new fortune for himself, he had not only made the name of Barnum loom larger than ever across the world of show business; he almost single-handedly had turned unmusical America into a music-conscious, music-loving country. This was an accomplishment that might well have capped the career of a lesser man, but for Barnum it was only an incident. For him, there were ever new miracles to be discovered, ever new enterprises to be launched.

Chapter 9

Humbugged

New projects for making money always teemed in Barnum's head; and, as long as they were show business projects, they were almost invariably successful. But when Barnum left his special province and ventured into other fields, the results frequently were disastrous.

Merely to list Barnum's successes at this time is sufficient illustration of the infinite variety and ingenuity of the man. Even while riding the crest of the Jenny Lind frenzy, Barnum had had other ventures going for him. In 1849 he and Sherwood E. Stratton, Tom Thumb's father, had organized Barnum's Great Asiatic Caravan, Museum and Menagerie. They had chartered a ship and sent it to Ceylon in May, 1850; and it had come back loaded with a dozen elephants and other wild animals strange to Americans. Ten of the elephants, harnessed in pairs to a chariot, paraded up Broadway and were reviewed by Jenny Lind from the Irving House.

The Menagerie, including Tom Thumb as a special

attraction, then went on tour. It traveled the country for four years and yielded large profits to its owners. Then all the animals were sold except one large elephant. Barnum sent this animal to his Bridgeport estate and put him in a six-acre field next to the tracks of the New York & New Haven Railroad. A keeper gaudily dressed in Oriental costume was furnished with a timetable; and each time a train was due, he would get out the elephant, hitch him to a plow, and present railroad riders with the weird sight of an elephant industriously plowing a Connecticut field. The elephant plowed and replowed the field innumerable times as a living advertisement for Barnum and his American Museum.

The Museum continued to represent the backbone of Barnum's financial enterprises, and he continued to give it his closest attention. In August, 1850, he advertised that he was exhibiting a Negro who had discovered a magic weed that would turn all Negroes white. Barnum hailed this discovery as the solution to the Negro problem, and the press fell for the stunt, running daily articles describing Barnum's Negro and trying to decide whether he was getting any paler. Of course, he wasn't; but the debate swelled receipts at the Museum.

Barnum never let interest cool. As soon as he had worked his Negro with the white wonder-working weed to the limit, he presented the public with something new. A beauty contest in which Barnum offered 200 prizes to "the handsomest women in America" was a sensation; so was a baby show. All of these attractions were eclipsed, when in July, 1853, Barnum exhibited the Bearded Lady.

[*142*]

According to a pamphlet issued at the time, the bearded one had been born in Switzerland in 1831 and had had a slight down on her face even as a baby. At the age of eight, she had a beard two inches long, and this grew to be five inches long by the time she was fourteen. The Bearded Lady had been exhibited in France with great success and had been presented to Louis Napoleon. She had toured England, where she was said to have drawn some 800,000 spectators. When Barnum placed her upon the stage of the American Museum, New Yorkers flocked in droves to see the strange sight of a lady with hair on her face.

With success seeming to crown his every effort, Barnum took time out in the summer and fall of 1854 to write the first edition of his autobiography, entitled *The Life of P. T. Barnum Written by Himself*. It was, to say the least, a most unusual book. Barnum was frank, perhaps not completely frank, but still so frank that he shocked and outraged important personages who did not like to be reminded how easily they had been duped. Especially offended were the newspapers. Barnum, in high glee, described the manner in which consistently he had "worked" the press by planting stories to whip up controversy and interest in even the most questionable of his promotions, such as Joice Heth and the Fejee Mermaid. The result was that the press was shown up to be both ignorant and gullible. And, naturally, the press didn't like it.

Editorial brickbats flew at Barnum from all directions, but these only served to advertise his book. The public, naturally curious to discover what the furore was all about, bought the book in great numbers and ate up Barnum's revelations with enthusiasm. The *Life* became a great popular success, and from 1855 until he died, Barnum periodically revised it, adding new chapters as his career progressed.

The effect of the book was tremendous and far-reaching, for it presented in engaging terms a success formula that justified the American businessman in almost everything that he did. Barnum made no pretense. He gloried in his title, The Prince of Humbugs, described how he had duped press and public, and calmly took the attitude that success justified the means. He had been reared in the hard school of the New England storekeeper, a school in which buyer and seller had to be equally wary of each other. Each knew the other was out to "skin" him, and the one who wound up doing the "skinning" was the better, the cleverer man. It was that simple.

Barnum took great satisfaction in his own cleverness, and he was no hypocrite. He did not deny, as so many more pompous souls did, that he had done what he had done; instead, he bragged about it. "There's a sucker born every minute," he said in a speech at the time. The prevalence of suckers wasn't the smart man's fault; but the smart man would be a sucker, too, if he ignored this fact of life. The suckers had been put on earth to be taken advantage of, but the trick was that you must take advantage of them "honestly." By this, Barnum meant that you must offer the sucker *something;* you musn't rob him outright. This, to Barnum's mind, represented the great difference between innocent "humbugging" and all-out dishonesty. The Fejee Mermaid might have been a fraud, but the suckers who were lured into the American Museum to see this fraud really got their money's worth once they were inside. Barnum showed them real animals, legitimate marvels of the world, and if the public had to be teased and tempted to partake of the fare he offered, that was all right. It was all for the public's own good in the end.

Such was Barnum's philosophy. By clearly expressing it in his book, by revealing many of his tricks of promotion, he had an impact on his time far beyond that of any ordinary showman. He was the pioneer, the spiritual father, of what has become today the multi-billion dollar advertising and publicity business. The entire gaudy, often phony, world of Madison Avenue owes a debt to Barnum and the *Life* he wrote that showed it the way. American business was similarly in his debt. Barnum's saying, "There's a sucker born every minute," became one of the most famous quotations in the language. The business world appreciated its truth, and it loved the way Barnum rationalized taking advantage of the sucker for the sucker's own good under a banner reading "Honesty is the Best Policy." You took advantage of the sucker to achieve success, and everything you did was highly moral. The businessman could eat his cake and have it, too. He liked that.

The result was that while editors howled because Barnum had given away his trade secrets and exposed them as credulous fools, many important businessmen took Barnum to their hearts. He was cut of the same cloth; he had made every trick of trade respectable. And, oddly enough, even the suckers liked him. They liked his wit, his engaging personality, his bald candor. They would have liked to be so clever themselves; they would have liked to be Barnum.

It was a reaction that, of course, delighted Barnum. He sat back in his study at Iranistan, and chuckled over his success as an author and watched the receipts at the American Museum continue to grow. But now, at the height of success, came the first faint rumblings of disaster.

The shocking fact was that Barnum was a terrible businessman. In show business, every act he touched returned the clank of gold; but when it came to studying a balance sheet or handling the intricacies of corporate finance, he was lost. Almost every time he ventured outside his own special field, he lost, either a little or a lot. He put money into a fire extinguisher that didn't extinguish. He invested in the steamship *North America,* but the steamer couldn't find enough passengers and freight to make a profit. He financed the *Illustrated News,* a weekly New York newspaper that expired after a year simply because Barnum's partners knew next to nothing about running a newspaper. These mishaps had taken little more than flea bites out of a fortune as huge as Barnum's, but now Barnum became involved in a transaction that took the whole hog.

Always an ardent Bridgeport booster, Barnum envisioned a great expansion for the area; and so, in 1851, he went into partnership with William H. Noble, a wealthy Bridgeport businessman, in the purchase of 224 acres of land on the east side of the Pequennock River. Here Noble and Barnum dreamed of building a new, model community to be known as East Bridgeport. They planted trees, set aside an eight-acre grove as a park, laid out roads, and built a toll bridge connecting their new town with the parent city. A coach manufacturer established his factory in the new community; and Barnum, in his enthusiasm, scattered money prodigiously in an effort to finance new enterprises for his town.

He was in this reckless spending mood when the Jerome Clock Company of New Haven, then the largest clock manufacturers in the nation, came to him looking for financial aid. The company, Barnum was told, was having some purely temporary difficulties, but a loan from Barnum would cure all. A bank official certified that Jerome Clock was a noble outfit run by fine people; and Barnum, taking him at his word, agreed to go security on $110,000 worth of the company's notes. He made just one stipulation: the company, as soon as possible, would move its factory, employing 700 workers, to his model community of East Bridgeport.

Jerome Clock officials were only too happy to make this promise, one that they apparently never had any intention of fulfilling; for the clock factory remained in New Haven and the clock officials nibbled away at Barnum's money. Just what happened, just who was responsible, never did become clear. Only Barnum's recklessness was obvious. He signed blank notes so that the firm could use them as needed; he signed new notes, and apparently larger notes, when old notes were retired; he became so involved that he lost sight of the $110,000 limit he originally had imposed; and by the fall of 1855, when the Jerome Clock Company collapsed and went into bankruptcy, Barnum found that he had written his signature on $500,000 worth of paper. He was responsible, he would have to pay—and he couldn't. He, too, went into bankruptcy.

Iranistan was lost; all his holdings, all his fortune was swept away. The downfall of Barnum, coming virtually on the heels of the publication of the *Life* in which he had told the tale of his success, created a sensation throughout the nation. Newspapers that had smarted at his disclosures now chortled happily all over page one and pointed out that there was, after all, a justice for such rogues. The happiest editor in the land was undoubtedly James Gordon Bennett, whom Barnum had exposed in the *Life* for being doubly humbugged by the stories Levi Lyman spoon-fed him in the Joice Heth episode. In an editorial on March 17, 1856, Bennett commented gleefully on Barnum's downfall and concluded that this was "a case eminently adapted to 'point a moral or adorn a tale.'"

Bennett's view was not, however, the universal one. Barnum had his friends. Some of the most prominent businessmen of the day, corporations, hotels, actors, actresses, singers, civic officials offered to rescue him with gifts, loans, a series of benefit performances. The citizens of Bridgeport held a mass meeting and offered to raise $50,000; other friends offered to raise a $100,000 fund by subscription. But Barnum refused all offers of aid. He was grateful, he said, but he had never asked anything "of the public on personal grounds." He still had his health; he was still able to work; he would make his own livelihood for himself and his family.

It was a courageous and commendable stand, but perhaps it was not quite as noble as Barnum made it appear. For the truth was that Barnum, though he had been hardhit, had not been totally wiped out. He was bankrupt, yes, as far as any funds or property that he personally controlled;

but he had had the foresight, as have so many businessmen before and since, to put a sizeable portion of his holdings in his wife's name. These were *hers;* they could not be attached to satisfy *his* debts. And so, no matter what happened, Barnum wasn't going to starve.

Just how much of a fortune Mrs. Barnum held never was definitely established. One valuable bit of paper that indisputably was in her name was the lease of the American Museum. The stock of the Museum had to be sold—and Barnum arranged the sale to two of his former managers at double the original cost of his collection—but the lease, which brought an income of $19,000 a year, remained the property of Mrs. Barnum. There are indications that Barnum had squirreled away other large sums in her name. Later, when he went to England, the great English novelist, William Makepeace Thackeray, offered to aid him; but Barnum refused the offer, remarking that he was in no danger of needing for his daily bread as "my wife is worth 30,000 or 40,000 pounds." This would be some $200,000 in American money, and Thackeray was properly startled by the figure. "Is it possible?" he asked. "Well, now, you have lost all my sympathy. Why, that is more than I ever expect to be worth; I shall be sorry for you no more."

To be overly sorry for Barnum, it appears, would indeed have been wasted sympathy; yet his experience, even if he was not quite the pauper he pretended to be in public, was both ugly and humiliating. For months, he was badgered by lawyers and compelled to testify in a long succession of hearings whose object was to try to uncover additional resources that might be attached to satisfy his creditors. This

[*149*]

constant harassment and heckling won him much sympathy among the press and public, and there was general amusement when Barnum turned on his tormentors, as he often did, and made them look foolish.

One day he was being questioned by a lawyer who demanded to know what was his present business. "Attending bar," Barnum said.

"Attending bar! Attending bar!" cried the lawyer. "Why, I thought you were a teetotaler."

"So I am," said Barnum.

"And yet, sir, you have the audacity to assert that you peddle rum all day and drink none yourself?"

"That is not a relevant question," said Barnum.

The judge told him that he must answer.

"Very well," said Barnum, "I do attend bar, and yet never drink intoxicating liquors."

"Where do you attend bar, and for whom?" snapped the lawyer.

"I attend the bar of this court nearly every day, for the benefit of two-penny lawyers and their greedy clients," snapped back Barnum, pulling the rug out from under his tormentor to the great delight of the entire courtroom.

The hearings finally dragged to an end, but even before they did, Barnum had begun to plan for the future. Shortly after he went into bankruptcy, the Wheeler & Wilson Sewing Machine Company bought property in East Bridgeport and established a large factory there. Barnum saw in this a clear indication that his pet real estate project was a valid one; and, though he had lost all his East Bridgeport property in his private financial disaster, he now borrowed $5,000 and bought some of the land back from his creditors. This property, in the end, was to bring him more money than the fortune he had lost in the Jerome Clock Company failure.

When the last lawyer in the bankruptcy cases had asked the last question, Barnum began to search for a way to pay his debts; for he was determined to pay them to the last dollar. Among the many faithful who had written him offering aid in his time of trouble had been the greatest of the little men, General Tom Thumb. The General had been about to set out on his own on a tour of the West when he heard of Barnum's misfortune; and he had written at once, offering to scrap all his plans and come to New York to take part in exhibitions for Barnum's benefit. Barnum didn't take advantage of the offer at the time; but early in 1857, having put his affairs in temporary order, he arranged to take General Tom Thumb and Cordelia Howard, a midget whose Little Eva in *Uncle Tom's Cabin* had made a hit in America, on a long tour of England and the continent.

This venture turned out to be almost as successful as the first trip that Barnum and General Tom Thumb had made abroad. Everywhere they went, Barnum was warmly received; and everywhere the General and Cordelia Howard drew huge crowds. Barnum was soon sending home thousands of dollars to pay off his debts and buy back some more of his lost Bridgeport real estate. Tom Thumb was by now an expert showman in his own right, and Barnum quickly discovered that the tour of the two midgets was practically running itself with little need of supervision on his part. Therefore, he began to cast about him for a more profitable means of employing his time.

Some of his English friends had suggested that he should go on tour himself with a lecture, "The Art of Money-Getting." The title, under the circumstances, struck Barnum as highly humorous. He thought to himself, he wrote, that the lecture would be more appropriately titled, "The Art of Money-Losing"; but since people are interested in getting money, not in losing it, he resolved to give the money-getting theme a try. His lecture was an immediate success and made Barnum a lot of the very money he was discussing. In 1859 he spoke in both London and the provinces, delivering the lecture more than 100 times. Late in that year, having reaped another fortune in England and the continent by Tom Thumb's efforts and his own, Barnum returned with his family to the United States and paid off all but $20,000 of his debts.

A mere $20,000 was nothing to daunt Barnum. He was practically solvent again in his own name, and he was ready to resume his career where he had been compelled to leave off. Everything, of course, would not be quite the same. Iranistan, which had been taken over by his creditors, was gone. Workmen had been refurbishing the huge mansion, one of them had left a lighted pipe on a cushion, and Barnum's great castle had burned to the ground. Though his home had been lost in this disaster, there was still the American Museum to claim his time and attention—and to rebuild his fortune.

The Museum had not been doing well under the direction of the two former employees who had purchased its curiosities from Barnum. The Barnum touch had been missing; and the Barnum touch, as Jenny Lind had discovered, made all the difference. The new operators of the Museum evidently realized this, for on March 17, 1860, they sold the museum collection back to Barnum. Barnum at once resumed full-time operation of the Museum in typical Barnum style. He renovated the entire building; he decked it out in brilliant flags and streamers; and he plastered the entire city of New York with flaming posters proclaiming, "Barnum's on his feet again."

The inevitable result was a truly Barnum-sized audience when he gave his first show on March 24, 1860. Appearing on the stage himself, he addressed his paying clientele on the topic of his rise and fall, winding up with a description of the manner in which he had triumphed over adversity. He told how frugally his family had lived, how hard they had struggled, how he had paid off all his debts. It just showed what a man could do if he had a little intelligence and guts and perseverance. The talk was sound American, poor-boy-to-riches stuff; and Barnum's audiences lapped it up. Almost in no time, crowds the size of those in the old days were flocking once more through the doors of the American Museum.

To keep his customers coming, Barnum exercised his well-known flair for always discovering something new and unusual to exhibit. He had been running the Museum for only about a month when he encountered James C. Adams, known as Grizzly Adams, a Western hunter and trapper. Adams had just arrived in New York from San Francisco with a boat load of 20 grizzly bears, several wolves and buffaloes, California lions and tigers and elk, and above all Old Neptune, the Sea Lion of the Pacific. Grizzly Adams had tamed these wild animals to obey him, but they hadn't taken kindly to the long sea voyage and one of his pet bears, General Fremont, had delivered a clout that had caved in the top of Adams' head. Adams had been told that he would die of the wound before long, but he felt that he had several good working months left and he wanted to make enough money to lay aside a nest egg for his wife before he departed. So he had come to Barnum.

Barnum promptly formed a partnership with Grizzly Adams. They set up a tent at Broadway and Thirteenth Street in which Adams could exhibit his menagerie; and on opening day Barnum put on a show that was to become familiar in later years to all lovers of the circus. He staged a colorful parade up Broadway. First came a brass band; then Adams' wild animals; then Adams himself riding General Fremont, the grizzly that had laid his skull open. The sight was a decidedly novel one in New York and crowds came to see Adams and his strange troupe of wild trained animals. After the New York exhibition, Adams took his menagerie on tour through the New England states, keeping to the road until he had earned the nest egg for his wife and the time came for him to die. When it did, Barnum bought his animals and added them to the Museum collection. All were later sold except Old Neptune, the Sea Lion of the Pacific, who lived on in a special Museum tank that was supplied daily with fresh salt water.

Hardly had the novelty of Grizzly Adams and his Wild West animals worn off before Barnum found a new attraction with which to lure New Yorkers. In 1861, he created a sensation by going to Canada and bringing back a pair of white whales to live in tanks at the museum. Unfortunately, neither he nor his employees knew anything about the care and feeding of white whales, and the mammals quickly died. Undaunted, Barnum had another pair of white whales shipped from Nova Scotia; and he kept the white whales coming until he got them at last to live. Thousands of New Yorkers rushed to see them.

No trouble was too much, no trick too tricky for Barnum if it would insure a good show. In 1864, ten of the most distinguished Indian chiefs in the nation went to Washington to pay their respects to President Abraham Lincoln. Barnum bribed their interpreter to bring them to New York first and exhibit them at the American Museum. The chiefs, proud men all, had no suspicion that they were being used as freaks to attract paying crowds; they supposed that they were being honored, as befitted rulers of their high station, when they were invited to meet the people of New York from the stage of Barnum's American Museum.

Barnum exerted himself to keep them under that happy delusion. After two public "receptions" at the Museum, he escorted the Indian chiefs to City Hall, where the Mayor made them a speech of welcome. At a public school, children gave an entertainment in their honor; and Barnum personally drove them around the city and showed them the sights of the town. But he always made certain that he got them back to the Museum in time for their next scheduled performance.

Barnum added spice to the exhibition of the Indian chiefs by a daring bit of byplay. One of the chiefs was known as Yellow Bear, and Yellow Bear had the reputation of hav-

The unsuspecting chiefs gave Barnum's audience many a laugh.

ing been one of the bloodthirstiest Indians white men had encountered in the West. Fortunately, Yellow Bear, like the other chiefs, did not understand a word of English; and Barnum, in introducing him, took advantage of this. Patting Yellow Bear on the head in his most affectionate manner, Barnum would turn to the audience and say:

"This little Indian, ladies and gentlemen, is Yellow Bear, chief of the Kiowas. He has killed, no doubt, scores of white persons, and he is probably the meanest, black-hearted rascal that lives in the Far West."

Once more Barnum would pat Yellow Bear on the head, and Yellow Bear, thinking he was being greatly honored, would smile and bow in pleasure.

"If the bloodthirsty little villain understood what I was saying," Barnum would continue, "he would kill me in a moment; but, as he thinks I am complimenting him, I can safely state the truth to you, that he is a lying, thieving, treacherous, murderous monster. He has tortured to death poor, unprotected women, murdered their husbands, brained their helpless little ones; and he would gladly do the same to you or me if he thought he would escape punishment. This is but a faint description of the character of Yellow Bear."

Then Barnum would give the chief another pat on the head; the chief would smile and bow again; and the audience would howl with laughter.

This scene was repeated daily for a week before the Indians discovered that they were really being used as a side-show that people were paying money to see. They were highly insulted and left the next morning for Washington, haughty in their injured dignity. Barnum breathed a sigh of relief to see them go. They had given him a wonderful attraction for a week without costing him a dime except for their keep and the bribe he had paid their interpreter; and when they left, they went quietly, without wrecking his Museum or attempting to lift his scalp. From Barnum's point of view, it had all been clear, wonderful profit. And the future held more of the same.

Chapter **10**

Romance Among the Midgets

Barnum's greatest successes were scored with the largest and the smallest of his exhibitions—the huge three-ring circus and the midgets. Probably no showman ever owed more to the little people than did Barnum. Beginning with Tom Thumb and continuing throughout his career, midgets were for him a never-failing drawing card.

It was in December, 1861, after Tom Thumb had helped him to reestablish his fortune and regain control of the American Museum, that Barnum was visited by a midget who promised to become Tom Thumb's rival. His name was George Washington Morrison Nutt; he was 17 years old, stood only 29 inches high and weighed a mere 24 pounds. Like Tom Thumb, his body was perfectly formed; he had a handsome head; and, best of all, he possessed a keen wit and a sharp tongue. Several other showmen were seeking his services, but Barnum outbid them all with an offer of $30,000 cash, plus all expenses, for the privilege of exhibiting him for three years. When the terms of this contract became known, the public promptly dubbed Barnum's new attraction "The $30,000 Nutt."

Barnum, as usual, made elaborate plans to promote his new midget-star. Having already bestowed upon Tom Thumb the army rank of general, Barnum now decided to even matters and show his perfect impartiality between the services by turning his new acquisition into a sailor and naming him Commodore Nutt. The Commodore was clad in resplendent naval uniform and outfitted in a manner suitable to his high rank. Barnum had built for him a miniature carriage in the shape of a huge English walnut. It had goldmounted harness, a miniature coachman and footman in livery, and it was drawn by two Shetland ponies. With Commodore Nutt outfitted in such style, Barnum followed his usual practice and advertised his presence upon the stage of the American Museum in huge posters that were plastered all over New York.

Great crowds came to see Barnum's new attraction, and there soon developed a most delightful complication. Commodore Nutt greatly resembled the youthful General Tom Thumb, whom New Yorkers remembered so well, and Barnum's audiences, eternally suspicious now of the devices employed by the Prince of Humbug, were determined not to be fooled. Commodore Nutt, they decided, was none other than General Tom Thumb in naval instead of army uniform. Barnum was simply trying to pull the wool over their eyes again!

This controversy—was Commodore Nutt really Commodore Nutt or was he General Tom Thumb?—stimulated attendance at the American Museum, and Barnum happily milked it for all the receipts it was worth. When the excitement threatened to die down, Barnum fanned it into a blaze again by re-engaging General Thumb. The General, who had grown decidedly more portly with success, had been on a Western tour of his own when Barnum first displayed Commodore Nutt; but Barnum now brought him East and put him back upon the stage of the American Museum. The master showman billed his new dual-midget attraction as The Two Dromios, and once more thousands of New Yorkers flocked to see the Commodore and the General. Even the appearance of the midgets side by side upon the stage failed to convince many of the skeptical. The Commodore, they said, was really General Tom Thumb, and the portly figure that Barnum was now labeling the General was really a tubby newcomer whom he had hunted up to humbug the public. With each viewer having his own firm and loudly expressed opinion on this momentous issue, attendance at the Museum soared once more, to Barnum's complete satisfaction.

Commodore Nutt rapidly became a famous little personage in his own right, just as General Tom Thumb had been before him; and in late 1862 Barnum took him to Washington to pay a call on Abraham Lincoln in the White House. The terrible Civil War was then raging; and when Barnum and the Commodore arrived, they found that the President was closeted with his Cabinet in a special meeting. Lincoln, however, being intensely curious, had left word that Barnum and the Commodore were to be shown in immediately; and so they were. The grim business of war was put aside for a moment, and the President and his Cabinet relaxed and enjoyed the smart sallies of Commodore Nutt.

When he shook hands with Secretary of the Treasury Chase, Commodore Nutt asked pertly: "I suppose you are the gentleman who is spending so much of Uncle Sam's money?"

Secretary of War Stanton spoke up, saying that he supposed he should claim the credit since most of the money was going for the army.

"Well, it is in a good cause, anyhow," remarked the Commodore sagely, "and I guess it will all come out all right."

Lincoln chuckled at this remark; and his long, lanky figure folded over as he bent to take the Commodore's hand.

"Commodore," he said facetiously, "permit me to give you a parting word of advice. When you are in command of your fleet, if you find yourself in danger of being taken prisoner, I advise you to wade ashore."

Commodore Nutt let his eyes rise slowly and significantly as they measured inch by inch the long-legged figure of the Rail Splitter from Illinois.

"I guess, Mr. President," he replied, roguishly, "you could do that better than I could."

It was a quip that made the President and the Cabinet laugh.

Barnum now added another newcomer to his troupe of little people. In Middleboro, Mass., he discovered a girl midget named Lavinia Warren, then just 21 years old. She had stopped growing at the age of ten and was only twenty-four inches high, weighing a mere twenty pounds. She had traveled in the West, exhibiting in a show run by a cousin on a Mississippi River steamboat, before Barnum learned about her and hired her to appear at the American Museum. He purchased jewels and an elaborate wardrobe for her and put her up in a suite at the Fifth Avenue Hotel. There she was visited by the most fashionable society of the day, including the Vanderbilts and the Astors, and a long roster of Civil War generals, including McClellan, Burnside, Rosecrans and McPherson.

When Lavinia Warren appeared on the stage of the Museum, Commodore Nutt and General Tom Thumb had ended their act; and the General was on vacation at his home in Bridgeport, amusing himself with his yacht and his horses. The Commodore, who was about five years younger than Lavinia Warren, was the only little man left on the premises, and he was promptly smitten by the charms of Barnum's new little woman. Lavinia, with a woman's perception, quickly diagnosed the Commodore's illness, and she confided to Barnum that she was worried about it; for, while she thought the Commodore was "a nice boy," she was a mature woman. Therefore, though she continued to treat him kindly, she carefully refrained from encouraging his attentions.

This was the situation when General Tom Thumb happened to visit the Museum one day to see his friend, Barnum. The General was introduced to Lavinia Warren, chatted pleasantly with her, and once she had left, hurried into Barnum's office for fuller information. He wanted to know everything about Lavinia, and in a perfect fever of excitement, he finally declared:

"Mr. Barnum that is the most charming little lady I

ever saw, and I believe she was created on purpose to be my wife!"

Barnum made no comment.

"Now, Mr. Barnum," the General continued, "you've always been a friend of mine, and I want you to say a good word for me to her. I've got plenty of money, and I want to marry and settle down. I really feel as though I *must* marry that young lady."

Barnum was amused and sympathetic, but he refused to take sides in the courting. The General must do his own wooing, he said, and he pointed out that the Commodore was going to be very jealous.

The General now abandoned Bridgeport, his yacht and his ponies. He stayed at his sister's house in New York City, and he haunted the Museum. Commodore Nutt resented his constant presence and was jealous of its obvious purpose. One day when the two rivals happened to be alone in a dressing room, he proceeded to show who was the better man by throwing the General flat on his back. This was humiliating, but the General, though he was older and more portly and slow, had the compensating advantages of wealth and leisure. While the Commodore was out on the stage entertaining Barnum's audiences, the General was backstage entertaining Lavinia Warren; and on Sundays and evenings when Lavinia was at leisure—and the Commodore was holding the fort at the Museum—the General was holding hands with Lavinia.

Convinced that his suit was progressing satisfactorily, General Tom Thumb persuaded Barnum to invite Lavinia Warren to spend a weekend at Barnum's new home, Lindencroft, outside Bridgeport. The Commodore, overhearing Barnum tendering Lavinia the invitation, asked eagerly if he might come, too. Barnum pointed out to him that he had to entertain audiences at the Museum, but the Commodore insisted that he could take the eight o'clock train for Bridgeport after his performance on Saturday night. Barnum, caught in the middle of this romantic tug-of-war between his two enamored midgets, could do nothing but let the Commodore come.

The timing of the two arrivals gave General Tom Thumb, however, a daylong edge, and he made the most of it. When Barnum and Lavinia Warren arrived in Bridgeport on Saturday morning, the General was waiting at the railroad station with his best coach and a coachman dressed for the occasion with a broad velvet ribbon and a new buckle on his hat. The General drove Barnum home and then took Lavinia for a drive. He stopped at his own house and showed her the suite of miniature rooms which his father had had specially constructed for him, filled with gorgeous furniture, midget-size. Then he drove the young lady to East Bridgeport and pointed out to her his real estate holdings there. Lavinia was much impressed. At luncheon that day, when Barnum asked her how she had liked her drive, she replied: "It was very pleasant; it seems as if you and Tom Thumb own about all of Bridgeport."

All day the General hovered about Lavinia Warren. He persuaded Barnum to invite him to spend the night at Lindencroft, although his own home was nearby; and after dinner he and Lavinia played backgammon. At nine o'clock Barnum yawned and announced he was going to bed; but someone, he said, would have to wait up for the Commodore. The General promptly volunteered, provided Miss Warren would wait also. Miss Warren, by this time, appeared quite agreeable to waiting in the General's presence.

Time was now becoming important to the General. The Commodore was due to arrive soon, and he knew that he had better work fast. He led Lavinia into a discussion of a prospective tour of Europe on which Barnum expected to take her in a couple of months.

"I hope I shall like the trip, and I expect I shall," said Lavinia. "Mr. Barnum says I shall visit all the principal cities, and he has no doubt I will be invited to appear before the Queen of England, the Emperor and Empress of France, the King of Prussia, the Emperor of Austria, and at the courts of any other countries we may visit. Oh! I shall like that; it will be so new to me!"

"Yes, it will be very interesting indeed," agreed the General. "I have visited most of the crowned heads myself."

He paused for a moment, sighed.

"But don't you think," he continued anxiously, "you'll be lonesome in a strange country?"

Lavinia didn't think she would.

"I wish I was going over," Tom Thumb sighed. "I know all about the different countries, and I could explain them all to you."

"That would be very nice," Lavinia admitted.

"Do you think so?" Tom Thumb asked eagerly, sidling his chair closer.

"Of course," said Lavinia calmly, in the most matter-of-fact of tone.

[*165*]

"I should like it first-rate, if Mr. Barnum would engage me," said the General.

Now Lavinia teased him.

"I thought you said the other day you had money enough and were tired of traveling," she reminded him.

"That depends upon my company while traveling," said the General, with quite definite emphasis.

"You might not find my company very agreeable," replied Lavinia, giving him the opening he sought.

"I would be glad to risk it," the General answered boldly.

"Well, perhaps Mr. Barnum would engage you if you asked him."

"Would you really like to have me go?" he asked, slipping his arm along the back of her chair.

"Of course I would," she said softly.

The General's arm found her small waist, encircled it, and drew her to him.

"Don't you think it would be nicer if we went as man and wife?" he asked.

Lavinia pretended to be flustered, surprised; she removed the General's arm from about her waist. But the General, talking swiftly now, put it back again, drew her to him, kissed her; and finally, with a happy sigh, she promised to marry him, if her mother would consent.

Matters in the parlor had just been so happily arranged when carriage wheels sounded outside, and Commodore Nutt, all eagerness, came bursting upon the scene. One sight of the General, already upon the premises and obviously in control of the situation, turned the Commodore's smile into a scowl, and he growled: "You here, General?"

"Yes," Lavinia replied. "Mr. Barnum asked him to stay the night, and we were waiting up for you."

"Where is Mr. Barnum?" asked the Commodore.

"He has gone to bed, but a supper has been prepared for you," Tom Thumb told him.

"I am not hungry, thank you," growled the disgruntled Commodore. "What room does Mr. Barnum sleep in?"

Told where he could find Barnum, he went stamping off upstairs in the worst possible humor and burst in on Barnum, who was reading in bed.

"Mr. Barnum," he demanded, "does Tom Thumb *board* here?"

"No," said Barnum sharply, "Tom Thumb does not *board* here. I invited him to stop over night, so don't be foolish, but go to bed."

"Oh, it's no affair of mine; I don't care anything about it," replied the Commodore grandly with face-saving pretense. "Only I thought he'd taken up his residence here."

And, draping his injured pride about him, he went off to bed. But hardly, it is to be supposed, to a pleasant sleep.

The Commodore had no more than departed when General Tom Thumb burst in. He jumped up and down in his excitement and cried out to Barnum:

"We're engaged, Mr. Barnum! We're engaged! What do you think of that!"

"Is it possible?" asked Barnum.

"Yes, sir, indeed it is, but you musn't mention it. We've agreed to tell no one, so don't say a word. I'm going to ask her mother's consent Tuesday."

[*167*]

Lavinia's mother presented no difficulty, but Commodore Nutt did. Lavinia didn't want to hurt him, and the General didn't want to be hurt by him. But how was this to be avoided? The lovers and Barnum discussed the problem the following Wednesday in Barnum's office, and Lavinia finally declared that she would tell the Commodore herself. The General retired from the scene, and Barnum summoned the Commodore. When he appeared, Barnum took command of the conversation.

"Commodore," he said, with a nod in the direction of Lavinia, "do you know what this little witch has been doing?"

The Commodore professed to have no idea.

"Well, she has been cutting up one of the greatest pranks you ever heard of," Barnum told him. "She almost deserves to be shut up for daring to do it. Can't you guess what she has done?"

The Commodore, with a stricken look, gazed at Barnum, and when he spoke, his voice trembled.

"Engaged?" he croaked.

"Yes," said Barnum, "actually engaged to be married to General Tom Thumb. Did you ever hear of such a thing?"

"It is so, Lavinia?" asked the Commodore.

"Yes, it is really so," Lavinia told him.

The Commodore turned pale. He choked, whirled on his tiny heel, and headed for the door. Pausing there a moment, he just managed to get out the appropriate wish: "I hope you may be happy."

The public announcement that Lavinia Warren and General Tom Thumb were to be married created a sensation in New York. Nothing like the romance of the midgets had ever occurred before to stimulate attendance at the Museum. Lavinia's receptions were crowded beyond capacity, and receipts soared to $3,000 a day. Eager to mine this romantic gold mine to the limit, Barnum offered General Tom Thumb, who was on exhibition with his fiancée, $15,000 if he would postpone the wedding for one month and continue their joint appearances.

"No, sir," the General told him excitedly, "not for $50,000!"

"Good for you, Charlie," said Lavinia, who was present, "only you should have said $100,000."

Having failed in his effort to prolong his best-paying romantic attraction, Barnum decided to see that his midget lovebirds had a wedding New Yorkers would never forget. The unforgiving James Gordon Bennett in The *Herald* attacked him for making a commercial spectacle out of the midgets' romance, but no charge could have been more untrue. The love affair, in the long run, was actually costing Barnum money, for he had to renounce Lavinia's European tour with its certain heavy profits.

In addition, he rejected all suggestions that he might make money out of the wedding and insisted that it should be a properly solemn church affair. It had been proposed, for example, that the wedding ceremony be performed in the large hall of the Academy of Music, with admission charged. Barnum spurned the idea. He made arrangements to hold the wedding in Grace Church, and he directed the issuance of 2,000 invitations to New York celebrities. Though as much as $60 was later offered for just one of these tickets

[*169*]

General Tom Thumb and his bride Lavinia were married in style.

of admission, Barnum himself made no profit. His only concern seems to have been a determination to see that his famous little people received the largest and happiest wedding possible.

The ceremony took place on February 10, 1863. Throngs gathered around Grace Church, and thousands waited in the cold for hours for the privilege of getting a glimpse of the diminutive bride and groom. Only the noted and the famous were permitted inside the church. Among them were the governors of several states, members of Congress, Civil War generals, millionaires, and families representing the social elite of New York. Indicative of the caliber of the wedding party were the names of some of those who sent the small couple gifts. President and Mrs. Lincoln, though they could not be present, sent "a gorgeous set of Chinese fire screens." Mrs. Cornelius Vanderbilt gave the couple "a coral and gold-set brooch, ear-rings and studs of the finest workmanship." Mrs. August Belmont presented "a splendid set of silver chased charms."

After the marriage, a reception attended by thousands was held in the Metropolitan Hotel. Two thousand boxes of wedding cake were distributed, and the wedding presents were placed on exhibition in the hotel parlors. In the evening, the New York Excelsior Band serenaded the bridal couple, and General Tom Thumb made a speech of thanks from one of the hotel balconies.

During their honeymoon, General and Mrs. Tom Thumb visited Washington, and President Lincoln gave a dinner and reception for them at the White House. After the honeymoon, they retired from public view for several months, but eventually they wearied of their seclusion and returned to show business.

They were highly successful. With Commodore Nutt and Minnie Warren, Lavinia's younger sister, also a midget, they toured Europe for three years, drew enormous crowds and made much money. This triumph was followed by a world tour that was also highly successful. In their private life, according to Barnum, the General and Mrs. Thumb were the happiest of married couples. They had one child, a girl who died at the age of two-and-a-half. The General himself died on July 15, 1883 at the age of 45; and although he had earned a fortune, he had spent so much of it on yachts and horses that he left his wife in relatively humble circumstances. Lavinia, sometime after his death, married Count Primo Magri, an Italian midget, with whom she continued on the exhibition trail for many years. She and her second husband later established a general store for automobile tourists in Middleboro, Mass., and this they ran until Lavinia herself died on November 25, 1919, at the age of 77.

Chapter **11**

The Circus

Barnum was now at the height of his fame and in the final stage of his career. He was known throughout the world as the magician of show business. Age was slowly overtaking him and almost imperceptibly slowing him down; but the name he had made famous was in itself worth a fortune and soon was to become the foundation stone of his greatest enterprise—the Barnum & Bailey Circus.

A series of misfortunes led Barnum to hunt for a new outlet for his energies and so brought him, by an indirect route, to the creation of the huge show that was to perpetuate his name for generations. In 1865, when Barnum was 55 years old, he entered politics. Originally a Democrat, he had become an ardent supporter of Lincoln, and a Republican; and he was elected to a seat in the Connecticut legislature.

He promptly locked horns with the New York & New Haven Railroad and defeated the railroad lobby in its effort to raise commutation rates. He was delivering a speech on this subject before the legislature in Hartford on July 13, 1865, when he received a telegram from his son-in-law, S. H. Hurd, that the American Museum was in flames. Barnum calmly laid the telegram aside and continued with the work of the moment—his scathing attack on the railroad.

Once the speech was finished, he hurried to New York and quickly learned that he was confronted with a financial disaster. The fire in the Museum had started in the engine room where a small motor was used to pump sea water for the aquaria. Smoke spread swiftly through the building, followed by the savage spurt of flames. Bedlam broke out. The live animals in their cages went almost wild. Monkeys jabbered, parrots screeched, bears growled, a kangaroo trumpeted his terror, and birds fluttered wildly against their cages. Firemen, watched by 40,000 spectators, tried to save some of the animals; but the fire spread too rapidly. One bear, an educated seal, some birds and a couple of monkeys were rescued; the remainder perished in the smoke and flames. When Barnum arrived, almost the first sight that confronted him was that of the burned, steaming bodies of two white whales that had arrived at the Museum only the previous week.

Barnum had had only $40,000 worth of insurance on his museum collection that, he estimated, had been worth at least $400,000. Assessing the loss, he was tempted to retire. His friend, Horace Greeley, urged this course on him, saying, "Accept this fire as a notice to quit, and go a-fishing." But Barnum had already discovered that he wasn't happy unless he was busy. Besides, he had 150 employees who had been put out of work by the fire; he felt responsible for them. He had also come to feel, after more than 20 years, that his Museum was a New York institution, an educational and amusement center that the city needed.

So he refused to quit. His wife sold the lease that they still held on the Museum site to James Gordon Bennett of The *Herald* for $200,000. Barnum invested the money, then hastily canvassed the world for new relics and curiosities. Before long, he opened a new museum at Broadway and Prince Street, but this museum was not so successful as the old American Museum had been. Barnum needed some exceptional show to revive public interest, and his hunt for this led him in the direction of the circus.

A man named Van Amburgh, proprietor of Van Amburgh's Menagerie, had acquired a reputation as the premier lion tamer of his day. He could make a lion and a lamb lie down together in one of his cages, and he sometimes introduced into the act a little child to lead them. Barnum conceived the idea of combining his museum with Van Amburgh's trained animals in one huge traveling show that would tour the country in summer and exhibit at his museum during the winter.

Barnum formed a partnership with Van Amburgh, and the combination proved highly profitable. But it lasted only a short time. On March 3, 1868, another disastrous fire burned Barnum's new museum to the ground. Van Amburgh's lions and tigers died in terror and pain, and Barnum's museum collection was wiped out. Once more, insurance did not begin to cover his loss, and he determined to retire. George Wood, the proprietor of Wood's Museum, offered him three percent of receipts just for the privilege of advertising that Wood's Museum was the successor of Barnum's. Barnum accepted the deal and withdrew to Bridgeport to brood upon his losses.

He had to find something to do, however, and so he bought more real estate, planted trees, laid out streets. Despite the fierce opposition of "old fogies," as Barnum called them, he developed Seaside Park, a beautiful tract of municipal land bordering on Long Island Sound. Beside this park, Barnum located his new home. Charity Barnum's health had begun to fail, and so Barnum sold Lindencroft and built a smaller residence named Waldemere, or Woods by the Sea, overlooking the waters of the Sound. Whenever he was at home, a huge white silk flag with the initials P.T.B. flew from the Waldemere flagpole.

Barnum was now well prepared for a pleasant retirement; but like many an active man before him, he soon found retirement anything but pleasant. He was restless, looking for something to do, for some new interest. And so when John Fish, an English friend and cotton manufacturer, came to visit him, Barnum set out to conduct Fish and his young daughter, Nancy, on a tour of the United States. They traveled to Niagara Falls, Washington, Cuba, New Orleans, California. In San Francisco, Barnum discovered another marvelous midget, whom he christened Admiral Dot, the Eldorado Elf, and whom he exhibited to large crowds for three weeks.

Back in New York in 1870, now 60 years old and still looking for some new and interesting enterprise to occupy his mind, Barnum became intrigued with the greatest show business project of his long career. He planned to form one enormous traveling show that would combine everything—museum, menagerie, and variety performance—under one set of tents. The idea appears to have been suggested to Barnum by two veteran showmen, W. C. Coup and Dan Costello, but Barnum quickly seized upon it. Coup handled the daily details of organization and planning; Barnum supplied advice and financial support and gave the endeavor the use of his name, a property now worth literally millions of dollars in show business.

The first Barnum circus, billed as The Great Traveling World's Fair, but soon to become known as The Greatest Show on Earth, opened in Brooklyn on April 10, 1871. The towering tents covered nearly three acres of ground. The show boasted the largest area of canvas that had ever been spread for a circus; it employed more men, horses, and animals than had any previous circus in either the United States or Europe; it offered wax works; dioramas; mechanical figures that breathed and gasped; Admiral Dot, the Eldorado Elf; and Colonel Goshen, the Palestine Giant, in whose hand Admiral Dot sometimes sat. Crowning all of these attractions were two eye-catching marvels—a family of true Fiji Island cannibals (at least Barnum vowed that they were true Fiji Island cannibals) and a giraffe. The giraffe was a splendid touch. Other circus managers had given up trying to exhibit this weird animal with the stepladder neck because the giraffe was a delicate creature that required much care and expense in handling, and then did not live long. Barnum reasoned that this made the giraffe a rarity, and he determined always to have at least one to display in his circus. Huge posters exhibiting the long-necked giraffe came in time to symbolize the circus itself, and to Americans it came to seem that the elongated giraffe was beckoning them to follow him and enter the world of the marvelous.

The Greatest Show on Earth was a tremendous success right from the start. Coup, like Barnum, was a master showman. He made lavish use of huge, flaming posters to advertise the approach of the circus, and these posters he plastered all around the countryside for a distance of 75 miles from the city in which the circus was playing. To bring in customers from this outlying area, he worked out arrangements with railroads to run special excursion trains; and instead of ferrying the circus from place to place by a cumbersome train of wagons, he devised means to ship the entire show—animals, acrobats, canvas tents—by rail. This enabled the circus to move faster, to cover more territory, to draw more customers.

By 1872, the circus had grown so huge that from 60 to 70 freight cars and six passenger coaches were needed to transport it. Wherever it set up its tents, practically all other forms of business stopped. One factory expressed its feelings strongly when it posted this notice: "Closed on account of the greatest interference on earth." No mere factory could hold its workmen to their tasks when Barnum's circus came to town.

The appeal was romantic, irresistible. First came the blazing posters to whet the curiosity. Then the long freight cars would roll slowly into the railroad yards and begin unloading their fascinating cargo in the romantic duskiness of early dawn. The huge, flapping tents that seemed to blot out the sky would go up, and then would come the parade, a spectacle of infinite allure—the steam calliope piping away; Oriental princesses lolling inside lurching howdahs on the backs of gaily caparisoned elephants; ungainly camels lumbering along; graceful, prancing zebras; yawning lions,

The circus parade drew young and old along to the big top.

snarling tigers, slinking leopards in their iron-bound cages; the giraffe and the grinning hyena; the cavorting clowns and the tumbling acrobats; the bewigged and powdered women performers in their flesh-colored tights. All promised sights such as few Americans had ever seen before, such as

[*179*]

few Americans could afford to miss. And few did.

In its first season, the circus grossed more than $400,000, and this did not include receipts from candy stands, concerts, and side shows. After the first year, business was even better. Soon the circus was taking in $1,000,000 every six months, and despite the tremendous costs of operation, the profits were colossal.

The secret of the circus' instant success, as both Coup and Barnum realized, lay in its sheer size, its sheer overwhelming magnitude. It was never-never land brought to earth under one gigantic spread of canvas; and so, in 1872, to increase the effect, Barnum and Coup added a second ring to their main tent and kept two shows in simultaneous, constant action. The two-ring show was soon expanded into the three-ring show, which was copied by every other circus in the business. It did not matter that no spectator, with a mere two eyes in his head, could possibly grasp all of the acts taking place in three rings at the same time; the mere fact that he was being deluged with more entertainment for his money than he could possibly absorb or enjoy made the circus seem like the world's most attractive bargain.

With the circus developing into the greatest enterprise of his life, Barnum went to Europe in September, 1873, to attend the International Exhibition at Vienna. While he was abroad, two momentous events occurred in his business and private life. First, Coup got him interested in constructing the first Madison Square Garden on the site of the old New York & New Haven Railroad depot at Madison Avenue and 27th Street. Next, in late November, 1873, while he was in Hamburg, Germany, Barnum received a telegram from his son-in-law, Hurd, telling him that Charity Barnum had died on November 17.

The blow appears to have been a crushing one for Barnum. He and Charity had been married for 44 years; and though her health had been failing, her death was totally unexpected. Barnum afterwards wrote that his "poor stricken heart" seemed to be breaking and that "the 'cloud' seemed so utterly black that it was hard to realize it *could* have a silver lining." For Barnum, however, the cloud did have a silver lining. He mourned Charity; but a year later he married Nancy Fish, the young daughter of his English manufacturing friend.

The years now unrolled for Barnum a swift pattern of successes. Coup, his health broken by overwork, sold out his interests in Madison Square Garden and the circus to Barnum; and Barnum, apparently indestructible, carried on, making the spectacles constantly larger and more spectacular than before. President Grant and members of his Cabinet, governors and judges, enjoyed Barnum's shows and congratulated him. Bridgeport honored him and elected him Mayor for one term. And all the time, the circus was getting bigger and bigger.

There were rival circuses, but most of these were so obviously inferior to Barnum's that they offered no serious competition. Only one gave Barnum real trouble, the Cooper & Bailey Circus, run by James A. Bailey. This gave Barnum serious competition, and Barnum made several efforts to buy Bailey out. Finally, in 1880, Barnum succeeded, and the two shows were merged into the famous Barnum & Bailey Circus.

The two partners were a fascinating study in contrast. Barnum was tall, strong and now, at 70, quite corpulent. Bailey, 27 years younger, was short, thin, alert and nervous. Barnum's disposition was placid, serene; he rarely worried. Bailey was a natural-born worrier. Barnum reveled in publicity, flaunted his title of the "Prince of Humbug"; Bailey detested publicity, wouldn't even let his picture be used in advertisements if he could help it, and detested every form of humbug, working incredibly long hours to obtain curiosities and effects that were genuine and unique. Together, Barnum and Bailey made the perfect combination. The flair of Barnum was balanced by the brains and skill and solid talent of Bailey.

This partnership had been flourishing for less than two years when Barnum pulled off one of the great strokes of his life—he purchased Jumbo, the second largest elephant in the world and the pride of all Great Britain.

Jumbo had lived in the Royal Zoological Gardens in London for nearly 20 years. He had been a small, ordinary-looking African elephant when he first came there, and he had grown slowly, as African elephants do; but he had ended up a perfect giant of an elephant. Only one elephant in the world was known to be larger, and that was one belonging to a prince in far-off India. Jumbo, in all the majesty of his prime, stood 11 feet tall. His legs measured five feet around. From tip to tip of his extended ears, he measured 15 feet. And he weighed seven tons.

With his ponderous gait, his massive slowly swinging trunk, his normally placid disposition, Jumbo had been a great favorite with Londoners for many years. Even Queen

Victoria and the Prince of Wales had visited him and ridden on his back, not once but many times. Barnum, on his visits to London, had often seen Jumbo and had always wanted to own him. But this seemed impossible.

In early 1882, however, with the Barnum & Bailey Circus booming to ever more fantastic heights, Barnum instructed an agent in London to inquire whether Jumbo could be purchased. Back came the surprising reply that the London Zoo would sell him for $10,000. Barnum at once dispatched the money. Jumbo was sold, and P. T. Barnum had him.

When the sale was announced, a storm of protest shook the British Isles. One might have thought that Barnum had stolen the British throne. Queen Victoria and the Prince of Wales urged the directors of the Zoo not to honor their contract with Barnum, not to deliver Jumbo; they even offered to make the British nation responsible for any damages that might result from a law suit. Poets wrote indignant verses. Children scrawled angry letters. Civic groups passed resolutions. Battered and beaten, the Zoological Society tried to plead in self-defense that its keepers had seen signs Jumbo was getting temperamental; it feared that he might have "fits of uncertain temper" and do someone harm, in which event they would have to kill him. They had preferred to sell him to Barnum. This explanation was smothered in a resounding chorus of boos; no one in Great Britain believed that huge, placid, friendly Jumbo, who had taken thousands of children for rides upon his back, was about to turn into an ugly and dangerous beast.

So great was the outcry that the editor of the London

Daily Telegraph wired Barnum, asking him on what terms he would give up Jumbo. Barnum, of course, had no intention of ever surrendering his prize. He wired back that "fifty millions of American citizens" were "anxiously awaiting Jumbo's arrival" and that even a "hundred thousand pounds would be no inducement to cancel purchase." Barnum had Jumbo, and he was going to take him to America.

In Great Britain, the hateful truth sank in, was slowly and reluctantly accepted. The British were about to lose Jumbo. Sorrowing throngs made final pilgrimages to the Zoo to bid farewell to the elephant who had come to represent in his massive person the pride of Britain. In one day, more than 4,000 persons visited Jumbo; and he was fed so many buns, a delicacy of which he was especially fond, that he almost died of indigestion. Jumbo, however, was made of stout stuff; he survived the kindness and the buns and presented Barnum's agents with a new dilemma: How was an elephant the size of Jumbo ever to be gotten to America?

The British were most uncooperative. They refused to let Jumbo be led through the streets, and so a way had to be found to crate and cart him. Did you ever try to crate a seven-ton live elephant? It is no mean task. Barnum's agent in London had a gigantic crate built of the stoutest wood, reinforced with strong iron bands. When finished, the crate stood 13 feet high and weighed six tons. Jumbo and the crate were introduced to each other, but Jumbo refused to have any part of it. He simply lay down and refused to move. The British were delighted; good old Jumbo, they said, he knew what was what. Barnum's agent was both frustrated and alarmed. How was he ever going to budge a seven-ton elephant that had made up his mind not to be budged?

Frantically, the agent cabled Barnum: "Jumbo is lying in the Garden and will not stir. What shall we do?"

From America, Barnum cabled back:

"Let him lie there as long as he wants to. The publicity is worth it."

Barnum was right. The publicity was worth it; and time cured the problem, as it so often does. Jumbo finally got used to the idea of the crate; he even became curious about it, ventured inside—and was securely fastened in his prison. Naturally, he objected. For an hour, in alarm, he bellowed and trumpeted and thrashed around, trying to shake his prison apart. He almost succeeded. But the stout wood and the strong iron bands held firm, and Jumbo eventually quieted down and accepted his fate.

The ponderous crate and its ponderous occupant, all 13 tons of them, were then mounted on wheels; ten powerful horses were hitched on to do the hauling; and Jumbo, in the gray dawn, began his last journey in England, a nine-mile trek through London streets to the harbor. Thousands of spectators lined the way. They gathered along the streets, in the windows of nearby buildings, on rooftops and along the wharves, waving to Jumbo and wishing him good-by. At seven o'clock in the morning, a pause was made and Jumbo had his breakfast. A lady admirer, who had followed him all the way from the Zoological Gardens, treated him to a large draught of beer for which, as for buns, Jumbo had cultivated a certain fondness.

At the waterfront, the last difficult steps were taken. Barnum's agent had had great difficulty finding a steamer with a hatchway large enough to permit a seven-ton elephant to be dropped through its deck into the hold. Finally, the *Assyrian Monarch,* a freighter with the necessary-sized deck opening, had been located and had been held in the stream, waiting. A large lighter was brought alongside the wharf to take the crated Jumbo out to the freighter. A huge crane hooked on to his crate creaked and groaned with the weight as it lifted crate and Jumbo from the dock and swung both down to the deck of the lighter. The lighter ferried its strange cargo out into the river; and there, once more, the freighter's tackle creaked under the weight as it hoisted Jumbo aboard and dropped him gently through the open hatchway into the hold.

With Jumbo went his longtime keeper, Matthew "Scotty" Scott. A bachelor, Scotty had cared for Jumbo for 17 years. He had become completely devoted to the great animal and spent his whole life in almost constant attendance upon him. He refused to eat with the other keepers, cooking his own meals and sharing everything with Jumbo, even whisky, beer and cuds of tobacco. During the long and rough 15-day voyage to America, Scotty stayed in the dark hold close by Jumbo's huge crate, and only when he slept was another keeper permitted to watch over the great elephant that had come somehow to represent the pride of two continents.

On Easter Sunday morning, April 9, 1882, the *Assyrian Monarch,* with her elephantine cargo, came up New York harbor. The event reminded Barnum of another just 32 years before when, on another Sunday morning, another ship from Europe had loomed out of the ocean mists, bearing Jenny Lind. Now, as then, he went down the harbor on a small boat to meet the ship; and despite his 72 years, he clambered nimbly aboard, his eyes sparkling with a boy's delight.

When he was led down into the dark hold and stood at last before Jumbo, he was moved almost to tears.

"Dear old Jumbo," he said. Then he added, doubtless for the benefit of the reporters who clustered around: "That beast cost me $50,000."

One of his assistants gagged at the figure and quietly corrected it. Actually, he said, the cost of buying and shipping Jumbo was closer to $30,000.

"Thirty years ago," Barnum rambled on, "I brought the biggest thing New York had ever seen up the bay in the shape of Jenny Lind, and she cleared $700,000 in nine months."

The clear implication was that he expected Jumbo to do as well. Ever the press agent, he wanted to make certain that the newsmen did not lack for vital details; and so he turned to the keepers and asked just how big Jumbo was.

"How high does he reach with his trunk?" Barnum wanted to know. "It's 49 feet, isn't it?"

"Twenty-six feet," answered a keeper, not yet trained in the Barnum school of publicity.

The old showman, the Prince of Humbug, laughed and shrugged off the correction.

"If I were a showman," he said, "I would have ex-

Jumbo became the biggest box-office star Barnum ever had.

aggerated it, but there's nothing like the truth."

Great crowds were waiting on shore when Jumbo was swung from ship to land, and a virtual municipal celebration was held. An admirer produced a bottle of whisky, and over the loud protests of teetotaler Barnum, the whole bottle was poured down Jumbo's willing throat. It was followed by a chaser of a quart of ale, and Jumbo didn't blink an eyelash.

Having awed the crowd with this demonstration, Jumbo was led up Broadway to Madison Square Garden. Here a new difficulty arose. There was no door wide enough to admit Jumbo and his six-ton cage. Both had to be left in the street all night while workmen labored enlarging the entrance. The next morning, the doorway having been sufficiently widened, Jumbo was wheeled inside and took his place in the circus. Instantly, he became the greatest attraction that the circus had. Crowds came to see him; and Barnum estimated that in the first six weeks he drew in an extra $336,000 in receipts, a performance that outdid even that of Jenny Lind.

For three years, Jumbo traveled with the circus all over the United States and Canada. Hundreds of thousands saw him, and Barnum and Bailey profited enormously from the drawing power of the most famous elephant in captivity. Then on September 15, 1885, in St. Thomas, Canada, while Jumbo was being led through a railway cut to board the circus freight train, an unscheduled freight locomotive came roaring down upon him. Scotty and the other attendants, together with a smaller elephant, managed to leap to safety; but huge Jumbo was not so agile. He and the locomotive met headon in a mutual disaster. The locomotive was wrecked, its engineer killed, its cars derailed. Jumbo's skull was fractured, and he suffered internal injuries. Collapsing across the tracks, he breathed one great, gusty sigh—and died.

The tragedy made headlines throughout the world, and it deprived Barnum, at one stroke, of his greatest circus attraction. Desperately, Barnum tried to salvage an exhibit.

He had Jumbo's huge hide stuffed and preserved by a taxidermist; and for years he continued to exhibit the massive figure of Jumbo along with another elephant, Alice, whom he had imported from England and whom he billed as "Jumbo's Widow." When this dual attraction began to lose its drawing power with the public, Barnum presented the stuffed figure of Jumbo to Tufts College, which he helped to found, and the college adopted as its emblem the head of Jumbo.

Before Jumbo was killed, Barnum had been making elaborate plans to take the circus and the elephant that had been the pride of England on a tour of Europe. Jumbo's death temporarily shelved the project; but in 1889, at Bailey's urging, Barnum and the circus went to London. The physical feat of crating and shipping such a mammoth show was so herculean a task that it generated reams of genuine publicity. The circus was constantly in the headlines; and in England, where he had always been liked, Barnum was welcomed as the hero of show business.

Great banquets were held in his honor; and every afternoon and evening when he appeared at the show, the entire performance stopped as he drove around the ring, pausing at times to call out to the audience in his aging, squeaky voice: "I suppose you all come to see Barnum. Wa-al, I'm Barnum." It was in some ways the best part of the show. Everyone did indeed want to see Barnum, a human phenomenon in his own right, and men waved their hats to him and ladies their handkerchiefs. This winter in London, when he was nearly 80, marked Barnum's last great triumph.

There was now the stoop of age to his broad shoulders, but his mind was as keen and wily as ever. One day, shortly after he returned to America with the circus, he tripped over a rope in Madison Square Garden and suffered a slight fall. Picking himself up, he cried out: "Where's the press agent? Tell him I've been injured in an accident!"

Deliberately, he spent a few days at home, and all the newspapers printed accounts of how Barnum had been "seriously injured" in a "painful accident."

In November, 1890, however, when Barnum was more than 80, his great physique began to weaken. He suffered a stroke and was in bed for three weeks. Physicians decided he could not recover, and Barnum was inclined to agree with them. He made preparations for the end. Carefully, he drew up a will. To make certain its provisions would be kept, he had himself examined by a number of doctors, all of whom attested he was of sound mind. Then he set aside a sum of $100,000 to cover legal fees, should any of his heirs try to break the will. Having thus made certain that his wishes would be kept, he disposed of an estate valued at some $10,000,000. A large portion of it he set aside to help finance the Barnum & Bailey Circus, the achievement that, he recognized, would keep his name alive for future generations. With the rest, he provided for his family, his children and his grandchildren.

Having made these plans, having provided for the erection of a great bronze statue of himself in his beloved Seaside Park overlooking Long Island Sound, he revived for a time and was able to move about his home at Walde-mere. But he did not go out. He did not have the strength. The iron constitution that had carried him through a long and busy lifetime with hardly a serious illness was wearing out, and Barnum knew it. Three days before his death, he said to his secretary: "Ben, I'm going to die this time."

The secretary objected, but Barnum interrupted: "No, Ben, I'm going to die."

There was a moment's painful silence, then Barnum matter-of-factly said: "I say, Ben you'd better see a con-tractor about putting up some houses on those shore lots. I've got too much money in the bank, Ben, too much money in the bank."

"Why, Mr. Barnum," exclaimed the surprised secre-tary in spite of himself, "you just said you were going to die!"

"Yes, Ben, yes," Barnum answered, "but I ain't dead yet, Ben, am I?"

It was the last brave effort, the last gesture of the Prince of Humbug. Early on the morning of April 7, 1891, he lapsed into unconsciousness, and at half-past six in the evening, as the April sun was setting across the waters of the Sound, he breathed his last. His greatest show was over.